KU-156-205

GRIMSBY COLLEGE
LIBRARY
OF TECHNOLOGY

Neofurniture

Neofurniture

Claire Downey

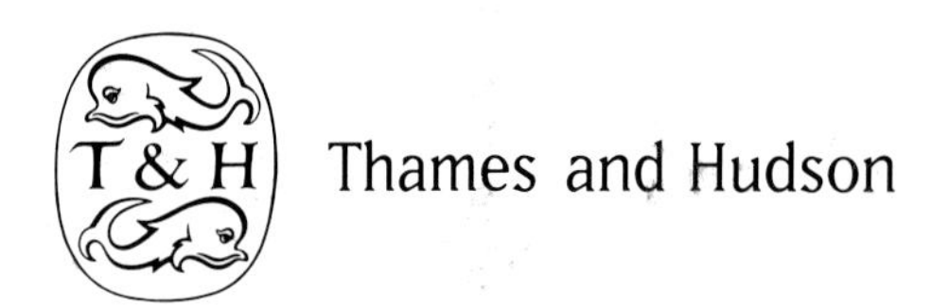

FOR MY PARENTS

First published in Great Britain in 1992 by
Thames and Hudson Limited, London

Frontispiece : Salvaged-metal chair, Tom Dixon, 1986, produced in a limited edition by the artist. Photograph courtesy of Tom Dixon.

Designed by Pamela Fogg

Printed and bound by Tien Wah Press, Singapore

Contents

Acknowledgments

A special thanks to the following people for helping to make this project a reality: Mr. and Mrs. Hans Beerkens, Eric Bonnin, Atelier Special d'Architecture, David Kimzey, Jean-Franck Lenfant, and Alice Stevens. I am grateful also for the assistance of all of the designers, galleries, and manufacturers who gave so much of their time and materials to this project, particularly Neotu and VIA.

Opposite: Cord chair, Christian Astuguevieille, 1989, produced in a limited edition by the artist. Photograph by Laziz Hamani.

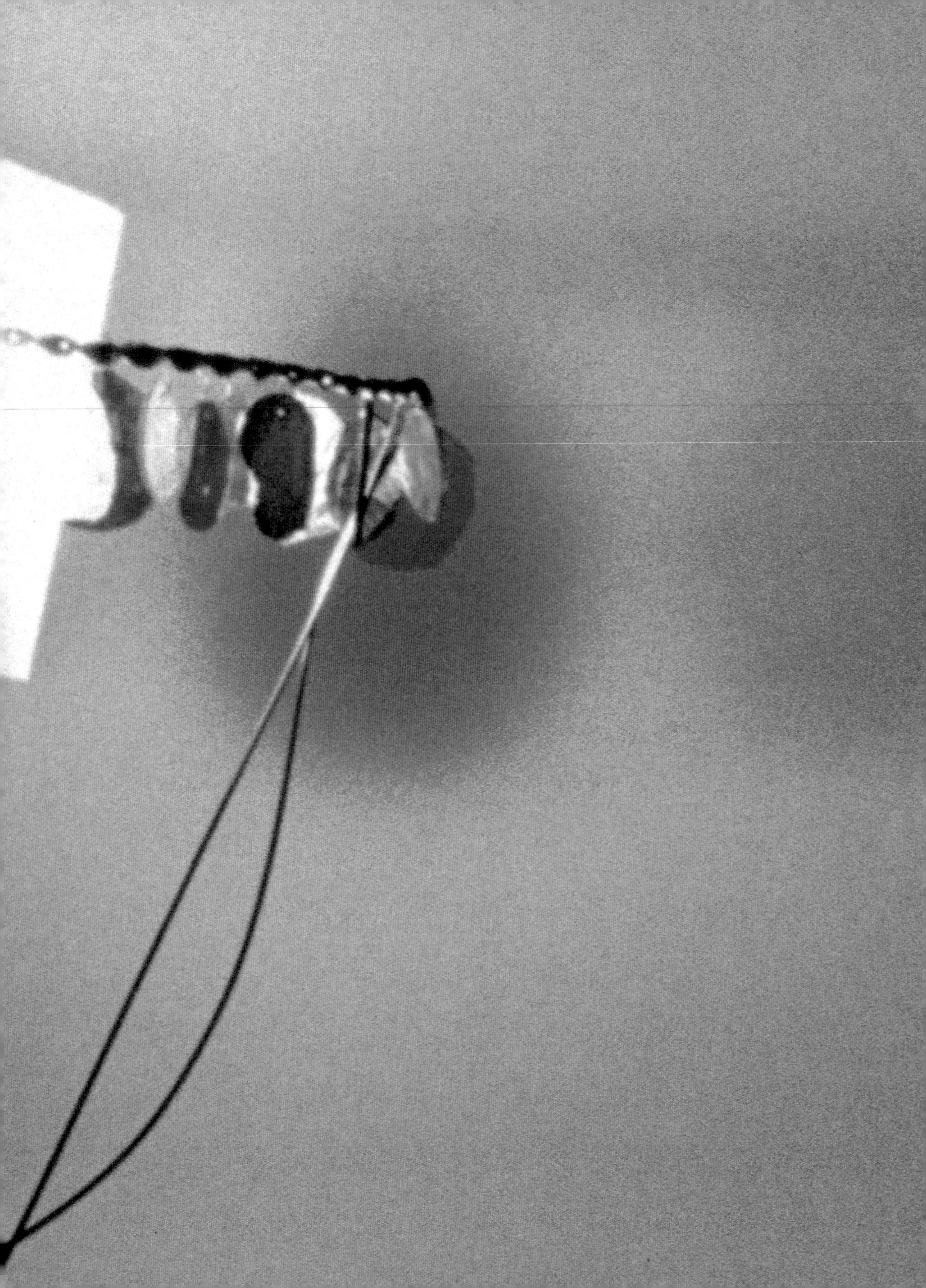

Introduction

The New Design, A Turn-of-the-Century Phenomenon

The turn of a century—a hundred-year division which serves so conveniently as a marker of change—is a time of eclecticism and nervous expectation. To the designer, making a way in a profession that did not exist before this century, the advent of the twenty-first century offers a chance to evaluate how far design has come and to estimate where it is going. European design, particularly self-searching at this moment, is a mélange of all the ideas of the past century. The aesthetic that makes some sense, or some*thing,* out of these random ideas will take the lead into the next century. So far, a compatible dialectic between the concerns of the individual and the attraction to spectacle dominates, yet new ideas are in the air. European designers are reevaluating both their relationship to the tradition of craft, which is their legacy, and their relationship to current culture—media, difference, exploitation, and rising social consciousness—which is their present. They have added a narrative to their designs in order to communicate on multiple levels. It is this layering of a narrative on the origins of twentieth-century design that marks the birth of the New Design in Europe.

Europe is in a state of change. In 1989 the Berlin Wall came down. The wall was a symbol both of a divided people and of an ideology that sought to limit, to lock in. As these walls crumbled, ideas began to circulate; Europe is now starting to assimilate the thinking of its eastern half. It is also planning to come together as a united Europe. There are new energies and many strong economies in Europe, which hopefully together can resuscitate much of European design.

In an effort to define, one can even say to celebrate, the current state of eclecticism in European design, Italian designer Andrea Branzi and François Burkhardt of the Centre Georges Pompidou in Paris organized in March 1991 the exhibition "Capitales Européennes du Nouveau Design: Barcelone, Düsseldorf, Milan, Paris." These cities were not presented as the only European capitals in which design was flourishing (a 1990 exhibition had focused on London); rather, they were chosen because the design these cities have produced covers a broad enough spectrum to establish that Europe is in the phase the exhibition proclaimed as New Design. The idea, content, and the conclusions of the exhibition are closely related in subject, time period, and spirit to this book. For instance, the exhibition manifesto identified recent turn-of-the-century designs as distinct from the experiences of the 1960s and 1970s, giving the following definition of them: "New Design breaks the unity of languages to the profit of a simultaneous multiplicity of styles: from neo-primitivism to bolidism, from theatrical to brutalism, from abundant eclecticism to severe minimalism." The manifesto writers go on to define the New Design as "producing objects which have, above all, a communication value." They speak of a "sensory revolution" where the "object is not as much a reality to understand, as a presence to perceive our sensory and corporal impressions."[1]

To convey the sensory appeal of the New Design, the installation was experiential. It was, in fact, a microcosm of contemporary European reality, where the divisions are blurred yet continue to exist. The passage through the New Design became surreal. Four quadrants, one for each city, defined the exhibition; they were divided by two dark and even mysterious "streets," which intersected at a crossroads. Although Branzi himself was responsible for the overall concept of the design, each quadrant became a compact concretization of an approach to design by a representative of each of the four cities. Here, within the brightly lit cities, one saw the differing hierarchies of aims in relation

Opposite: *Sibari* table lamp (detail), Toni Cordero, 1990, manufactured by Artemide. Photograph courtesy of Artemide.

Right: *Collier de Perles* carpet, Garouste and Bonetti, 1991, produced in a limited edition for Galerie Yves Gastou. Photograph courtesy of Galerie Yves Gastou.

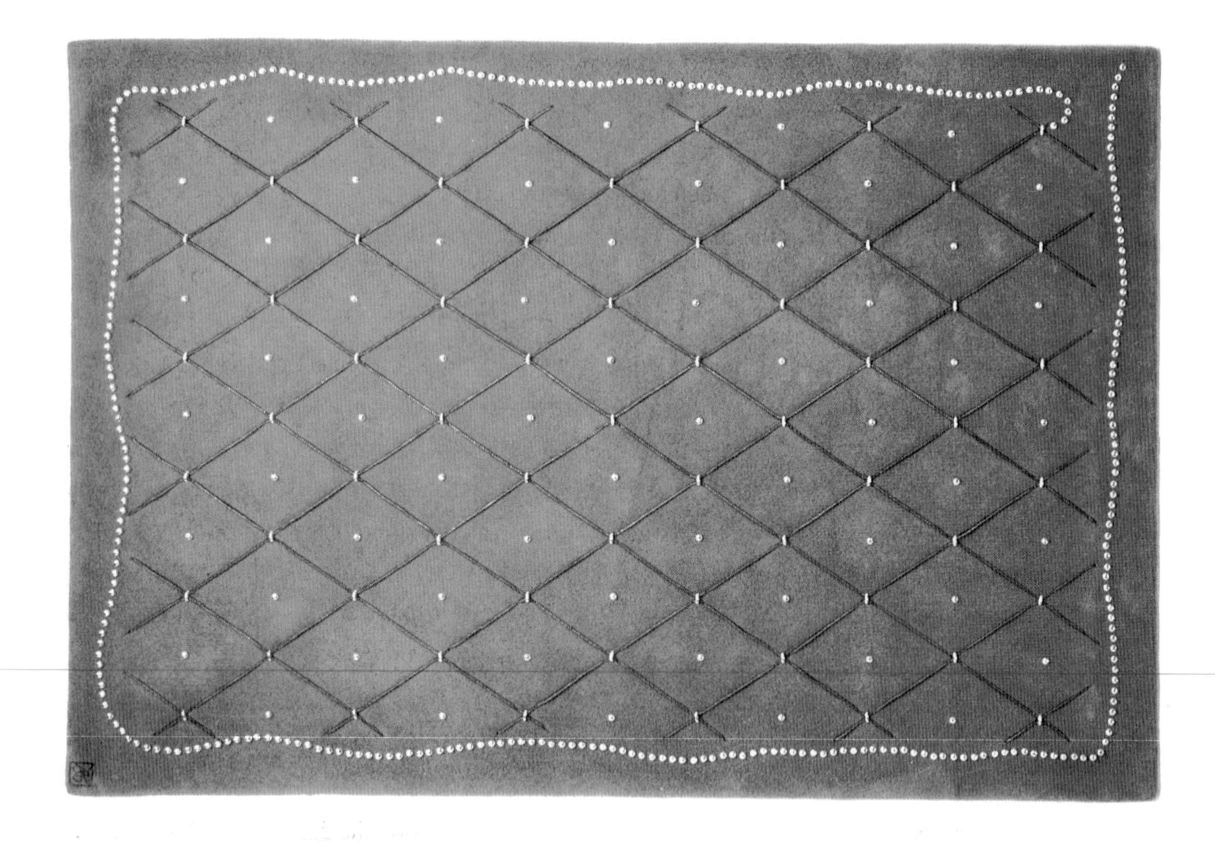

to the whole. Or, one could have looked at the exhibition as one city, with each of its quadrants offering a different perspective of the same organizing aesthetic; from the vantage point of the crossroads a shared spirit of communication, eclecticism, and a renewed sense of cultural relevance throughout Europe was apparent. In the broadest sense, the Paris exhibition was the "prettiest," with pastel colors and many small objects displayed in jewel-box-like cases, as in a museum. The Düsseldorf exhibition was more political, containing furniture with a message by placing S.M. Syniuga's chairs with images of Brigitte Bardot under the sign of a Mercedes-Benz star, or commenting on ecology with the rigid industrialism and *autobahn* divisions of Northern Germany. Milan had the most "constructed" exhibit, a room within a room, reflecting the architectural roots of the old guard of Italian design; this structure was often in contrast to those designs by an emerging younger generation who no longer fit the classic architect/designer mold. Barcelona chose to show designs solely in photographs displayed on walls like spread sheets from a magazine, and referring directly to a popular means of assimilating design today; below each image were actual details, or fragments from the finished piece, as if to say it is the technique, the knowledge of making, that separates a "design" from the merely attractive image. These four approaches, as much as the eclecticism of the objects themselves, demonstrated an ongoing cultural dilemma about how and at what level design fits into modern life.

The New Design, however, does not exist in a vacuum. Passing along the intersecting "streets" of the Pompidou exhibition, one encountered a mix of objects, furniture, graphic design, music, fashion design, and video, glowing in the dim light. The exhibition, with its many "expressive tendencies,"[2] just began to touch on the importance and influences of the different design and creative fields. These varying fields, figuring in the backgrounds of many of the designers discussed in this book, have produced the means of communication that have fused the New Design with current culture. At this point of fusion the New Design found its voice and, in fact, its popularity. "'The Nouveau Design' . . . favors the spontaneous urban expressions, the savage metropolitan dialects, opposes uniformity, the homogeneous brought about by the system of communication and of mass consumption."[3] Ironically, by not seeking to appeal to the majority, it has become more appealing.

There are dualities within the New Design which form the core of its identity. No single dogma prevails. At the heart of the New Design is the dialectic between image and content. Many cultural phenomena of turn-of-the-century Europe have collectively impressed upon a television generation that image is everything. In a time when top models have replaced the starlets as the girls to be emulated, it sometimes seems that we have lost even the necessity for words, that all can be expressed visually, in gesture, in a glance, in a styled image. One duality exists in the meaning of the visual message. Is it a message to shock or to seduce? Is it clever or garish? Is there a cultural or political message, a concern for the spiritual, the New Age, or is the message to satisfy the desire to indulge, to drown oneself in what looks and feels good? Whatever the meaning of the message, designers are using furniture to communicate at a conscious and physical level.

A strong image, at whatever level it speaks to us, can have more power than actual substance. In the New Design a disparity exists between those designs that become known and those that are available to the general public, partly due to a trend towards the one-of-a-kind object, or at most, the limited-production piece. What began as a means to get designs produced, even it if meant creating only one, has become the norm. Some designs, such as Garouste and Bonetti's early-1980s table based in a monolithic rock, have endured in small production with growing media attention. Each design publicized through the media reaches an international audience, though perhaps never leaving the city in which it was made. The media's reproduction of images visually replaces the assembly line. Volker Albus, speaking in a conference for the "Capitales Européennes" exhibition, remarked, "Products known visually are not necessarily consumed. They are, however, more memorable. A chair with a message is more memorable than one with no message done in hundreds of examples." Albus, who designed the Düsseldorf quadrant of the exhibit, is occupied with building the image of a new German design, or proving that something exists beyond the consumer image of efficient German goods such as the popular Braun coffeemakers. Certainly, the Bauhaus was not involved in reality, or with large production, but they did launch an image, one that would thereafter be associated with German design, with productivity, and of course, with Modernism. German designers such as Albus have today taken the position that in Germany there are two distinct cultures, which do not mix yet can exist together.

The many dualities of furniture design at the turn of the century include the calm versus the sensational, the New Agers versus the visual gluttons and fashionmongers, object craving versus a true appreciation of design, and the wavering between art and design. Those designers who work alongside the artisan, or who make the furniture or objects themselves, have often been called artists. Certainly, their one-of-a-kind creations are bought as art. Yet, with increasing frequency, these very same designers are working at the same time with large manufacturers to produce different but equally important designs. The dualities of the New Design often exist harmoniously within the work of one designer. Therefore, the dual nature of New Design is its normal condition.

Some dualities in the New Design are very subtle. For example, one tendency attempts to differentiate between the current rediscovery of luxury materials and handmade objects, and the idea of interior decoration. Fear of interior decoration as the image of trivial design—the opposite of "important" design—has made most of those who are not also architects opt for the title of "designer"; or if even "designer" seems too diluted for their purposes, they call themselves "artists." Yet, it is in the so-called dilution that the body of work becomes more interesting. Rare is the person working in only one medium. Most designers are sampling the full range of design, from glass production to forged iron, to textiles, to complete interior projects, which are not, of course, decoration. Without sarcasm one can say the state of design today allows a broadening of possibilities for the designer, who originates pieces and does not work as the decorator does, combining bits and pieces from the work of other people.

The dilemma is that many of the designs hanging perilously on the edge of a luxury goods market are sold in galleries and coveted as fashionable objects. One would wonder about design integrity if we were in the midst of the reign of the International Style; today, however, integrity is truth to oneself. Access to galleries means access to

Right: Forged-iron sofa, Eric Schmitt, 1989, produced in a limited edition by the artist for En Attendant les Barbares. Photograph courtesy of En Attendant les Barbares.

the gift of creation, experimentation, exploration, and indulgence. The shining machine—the assembly line of perfectly matched pieces—has lost its allure and romance. The New Designer retains a degree of fallibility, of elusiveness, and seems easier to trust. Rather than assume that good design is the property of all, we seem content with the inspiration of designs that are out of our reach, and allow for their existence alongside good, affordable, even the more mundane design.

One country particularly focused on a high-end design market is France. This book documents the rise of French furniture design in the new generation after Philippe Starck. Ten years ago, a book on European furniture design would have been largely an Italian story with few French designers mentioned. Today, movements such as the New Baroque are overwhelmingly French. The French have embraced diversity, detail, and even luxury, building on traditions from the eighteenth and nineteenth centuries and on a certain French affinity for the chic; sometimes the movement borders on a haute couture for furniture. Much of the success of French design can be traced to VIA. As the organization for the sponsorship of French design through collaboration with the French furniture industry, VIA, since its start in the late 1970s, has struggled to bring French design to world attention. They have sponsored the production of over 250 prototypes and have given Carte Blanche awards to designers such as Andrée Putman, Philippe Starck, and Kristian Gavoille. As VIA director Jean-Claude Maugirard explains, "While French furniture design was, since the 1950s, in a relatively calm period, the role of the artist has always been important to French culture. The rejuvenation occurred just at a time when the public was asking for more individual furniture, furniture which is not the same as what you see in, for example, an airport. The 1980s and 1990s announced the need for variety. The idea of diversity for a divergent public." This need has allowed the smaller French furniture manufacturers

Left: Hotel Otaru Marittimo, interior designed by Branson Coates Architecture, 1989. Photograph by Eddie Valentine.

to build an industry on limited production, which in turn has given designers the freedom to innovate. Limited production also means less financial risk for the manufacturer (a risk American manufacturers have not taken since the early days of Knoll). A progression thus occurs, from designer to artisan producer to—if successful—large manufacturer. "Designs which seemed at the start risky have become the basics in ten years," says Maugirard, "but only if this process has the means to evolve." The process is evolving throughout Europe, from what are practically cottage industries in London warehouses to the small, but high-profile, designer lines of large Italian manufacturers.

Along with this turn towards limited production, which has allowed designers to take risks, has come the rise of design publications which follow all the activity. These two concurrent trends tend to create a vacuum in the flow of supply and demand. What one sees in this month's design review is not necessarily available to the public. Gladys Mougin, who represents André Dubreuil and Tom Dixon in Paris, has long had to deal with disappointed buyers who want the exact piece they saw in a magazine, and do not understand why the designer will not duplicate the work (something that Dubreuil rarely does). Mougin has defined a new strategy for marketing design, which resembles that of an art gallery; she has a waiting list, and when, for instance, the newest Dubreuil piece arrives, the first on the list has the first option to buy. She also sells from the floor anything already in her shop, which is open to the public. Her strategy combines our habit of seeing furniture as something bought in department stores with a new awareness of design and designers. The important point is that the public, through exposure to design, has created a demand that the industry is not always ready to meet.

How much of our comprehension of the New Design is in the style of presentation, the packaging, the display, the publicity? Quite a lot. The layers of creation build from the early prototype, the exhibition, the publication, the eventual incorporation into the myth machine. Designers in the late twentieth century are not monks; they more than ever exploit the media. Often they have worked in other creative fields: music, clothing and jewelry design, video production, and set design. They see design as an activity that should be linked to movement, change, and the building of fantasy. Some have spent more time hanging out in clubs than in design schools. The street, the club, the music and fashion scenes of the late 1970s and 1980s were a formative ground for the designers coming into their own in the 1990s. It was there that they learned about people, rapidly moving images, fashion, and even social issues. The popularity of design is largely due to the profile of the designer. This new romantic figure, part creative genius, part streetwise poet, part businessman, is a person productively feeding the image machine; this profile is very attractive in the 1990s.

There is undoubtedly an aspect of fashion in furniture design, and therefore in this book, not only in the obvious inclusion of clothing designers (strangely, the only designers referred to as fashion designers), but also in the inclusion of furniture which itself sits on a fine—or not so fine—line between quick gratification and lasting design. The inclusion here of less rigorous design is intentional. No depiction of this turn-of-the-century period would be complete without an element of fashion, which pervades the current lifestyle. Fashion and, in some instances, even "seasonal" designs press for acceptability; they can also offer the public an awareness of design that might deepen with exposure. Exposure is the key word at the turn of the century, with its inundation of images, names, and the making of stars. Design also has its share of stars. People like Philippe Starck are recognized in clubs and restaurants, interviewed in fashion magazines and on television. Starck is an international designer and as such qualifies in current culture as a type of cultural critic. His every design is seen as a standard of "in." Starck sends drawings around the world by fax, spends excruciating hours in airplanes, and designs the places in which people want to be seen. There is not a large media machine behind Starck. He is the machine, and he seems to have an innate sense of how to maintain the momentum.

Starck, the point of departure for French design and already a household name, is not a major focus of this book. He is, indeed, a book in himself. Other designers of international reputation are discussed here, including those from other creative fields who have become the inspiration for designers of furniture today or who are designing furniture themselves. It seems that everyone is turning to furniture design, including clothing designers such Jean-Paul Gaultier and Rei Kawakubo of Comme des Garçons. Others, like Franco Moschino, are integrating their shop designs so closely with their clothing designs that the images become inseparable. Design has learned much about image and media, not to mention shape, color, and detail, from fashion; now, fashion is using design to strengthen its own image, to create the packaging.

The 1990s have seen a proliferation of design galleries in the European capitals, from Milan to Frankfurt to Paris. These galleries, as painting galleries before them, have shows and openings. The openings at furniture galleries, complete with invitations and champagne, have begun to attract unprecedented crowds, full of other designers, some serious buyers, and a lot of attractive, fashion-conscious people who have picked up on the fact that design is where things are happening. At the closing of the Borek Sípek opening at the Neotu gallery in Paris in 1990, the lights had to be turned off to disperse the wall-to-wall crowd, which overwhelmed Sípek's collections of glass and porcelain objects. Do these people even know who Borek Sípek is? Certainly some do, but this is not the point. The idea is to be seen, and exhibitions of furniture design have become the place to be seen. Why chairs and tables? Furniture design, easier to understand than abstract expressionism, is a new way in which the public can experience art. After all, most people believe they know about furniture, and most people will buy their own furniture at least once in their lives. They think that they have the ability to judge furniture; they know what they like and are less intimidated in choosing a chair than a painting. The advent of more interesting furniture, furniture that allows them to tie together their coveting of objects, materialism, and their love of fashion and of dropping names, is all the better. Magazines have proliferated, galleries have opened, people are buying, and many people are looking.

New Design, as it relates to our personal environment, our tastes, and ourselves, is a means of defining who we are. While the International Style might have sought to incorporate our being into a heroic uniformity, the New Design allows us the options to define ourselves as unique individuals. The nineteenth-century *flaneur* strolled the grand

European boulevards, drinking in the energy, the parade of fashion and manners, taking stock of how each person defined his or her status in society. The *flaneur* was the modern man of his time, the man chronicled by Charles Baudelaire and by the Impressionists. Today, one hundred years later, the modern man is again looking to invent himself, not as an observer but as a thief, picking through magazines, films, music, and the life of the streets to find the pieces to appropriate for a personal look and attitude. Foucault has said, "The flaneur stores memories—modern man extracts from images his modernity."[4] Unfortunately, the images are continually changing, one replacing the other, at an amazing pace. The task of producing oneself is work in a labyrinth. The home interior is where we have returned to enact our self-production and our sense of control. Today, fashion, media, and design combine to create a stage set for living.

The human aspect of the New Design is what makes it so appealing, its combination of domestic ritual and design aesthetic, of the tree branch with machine-made materials in a single chair, and the animation of furniture with animal or even human attributes. Furniture that is named *Lola, Wanda,* and *Diva* have come into our homes, as have tactile furniture and objects, and fabrics that recreate mythic tableaus. Designers tell us that their work was inspired by the dreams of children or by an imaginary princess. The New Design is sensual, fluid, alive. It is not that design has lost all sense of function; function is well understood. Rather, design has transcended functionality to move on to more emotional issues.

Why the modern man has chosen to embrace the baroque, an important element in New Design, has a great deal to do with self-indulgence and a return to spectacle. "The fact is that most of us have at one time or another come in close contact with a Baroque environment, and many of us have an instinctive liking for it,"[5] writes John B. Jackson on the subject of the urban landscape. He also touches on the difference between the viewpoint of the historic baroque, and what we are defining here as New Baroque. The New Baroque both incorporates the ideas of the baroque and contradicts them in its growing concern for the domestic and the individual. As Jackson notes, "I happen to admire a great deal about the Baroque point of view; I like its formality, its vigor, its humanism; I even have a certain sympathy for sound order that recognizes differences and puts them to use instead of pretending they do not exist." On the negative side, Jackson sees a "danger" in the baroque approach, "this disregard for private life, for the individual inner experience. The Baroque Age had little or no understanding of the importance of interior existence, speaking psychologically as well as architecturally, with the result that the age that came after it—the age that started before the French Revolution and lasted until about the Second World War—went to the other extreme, and emphasized the individual environment, at the expense of the whole city landscape." Jackson confines himself to the exterior urban environment and does not touch on the interior living space, which the New Baroque is indeed making much more personal, precisely because of the baroque embrace of difference.

The New Baroque is just one tendency in the New Design, but the emphasis on spectacle and movement which characterize it is also present in the other tendencies explored in this book. Many of the designers are found under several headings: The New Baroque, Primitivism, The New Naturalism. They are all modern, all trends of our time. A selection of designers discussed here are those who, involved in defining their modernity, have touched on what has long been divided into high and low culture. Here, all forms of cultural expression are considered valid, from the the museum piece to the music video. An attempt has been made to document this flourish of inventiveness at the end of the century and to break down many of the self-imposed borders of the new profession of Design. Just as Europe is facing change and redefining the function of its borders, design, which must reflect its culture, will break through its own isolation and join with other creative fields to communicate. Communication is the only true structure within the New Design.

Primitivism

Primitivism, more than any other design tendency that marks the eclecticism at the end of the twentieth century, points to the yearning for alternatives. So much was left unsaid in the gap between so-called high-tech modernism and retro-historicism that not only were there no options to choose from, but the tools with which to start over had been lost. Where were the poets and the artisans who could even begin to shape other possibilities?

Early in the 1980s, the French design team of Elizabeth Garouste and Mattia Bonetti, frustrated with the limited offerings of modern design, began to give shape to their own far more knowing vision: that of the noble savage. With tables based in monolithic rock, and chairs of forged iron covered with animal furs, Garouste and Bonetti unearthed a legacy of forms and textures uncultivated by designers up to that point. In fact, their designs were so new that, at the time, they had difficulty finding the craftsmen with whom to work; not because they required a new technology but because they had changed the expectations of the process of design—smooth functionality flowing off the assembly line was not their goal. Nor were they looking to be furniture makers in the crafts sense. They were designing furniture that would suit their projects—a Paris night club was one of the first—and that would be an outlet for their collective intrigues and dreams. In their worlds of feudal lords and fairy tales, Garouste and Bonetti struck on an emotionalism that ten years later would be at the center of a French design renaissance.

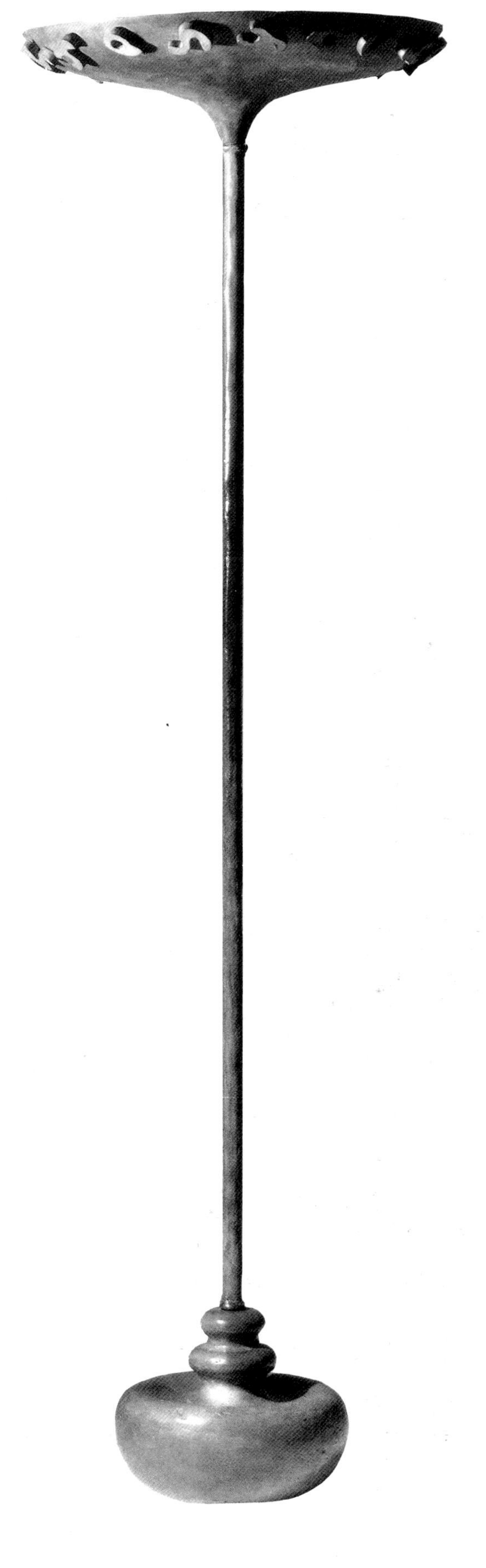

Opposite: *Sellette* forged-iron table (detail), Eric Schmitt, 1991, produced in a limited edition for Neotu. Photograph courtesy of Neotu.

Above: *Nuage* (cloud) floor lamp, Garouste and Bonetti, 1990, produced in a limited edition for Neotu. Photograph by Karin Knoblich.

The Primitivism of Garouste and Bonetti is not roughly assembled or conceived of by isolated artists unaware of the modern world. Just the opposite. The work is meticulously detailed and informed by a knowledge of art and culture. It is, in fact, luxurious design for an urban savage of the post-industrial age—a new modern hero. The inspiration is tribal spectacle, either jungle or urban. The very individual work of these two designers distills images from film, the museum, and the street and overlaps and reinvents them.

Primitivism is the creation of a history through an assembly of characters whose necessary elements—color, form, detail, and dress—recount the tales of a great passage. More often than not, this passage is through the imagination rather than a specific place or time; yet, it is more pro-active than escapist. For example, the *Afrika* table from the 1990 collection for Neotu is pure Garouste and Bonetti invention, or elaboration. The table's thick wood trunk is covered in oblong black knobs—breastlike ornaments—which add a legible characterization to a form that already recalls the image of Africa, but too abstractly, too mutely. In the same collection, the *Rodeo* desk and chair are more refined than the frontier ever was. This is the Wild West interpreted by two French creators as an image, an ironic inversion of frontier brashness paired with the elegance of its iron frame and smoothly fitted skins. This is Salon-Texan for bourgeois adventurers. The fact that these pieces are found in the same collection is a telling clue in deciphering the many faces of Garouste and Bonetti. Certainly, they are not concerned with homogeneity. No chairs were designed to go with the *Afrika* table, which is large enough for a dining room. "The choice of chairs," says Bonetti, "is left to the user." For Garouste and Bonetti, consistency is in the manner of interpretation, the process of seeing—in life, in the mind, in the act. Each design is a brief stop in this continual, visual journey. Each collection is a sampling of excerpts from an "on-the-road" film. The Primitive work of Garouste and Bonetti is always conscious of the realities that exist in the world today, but is never imprisoned by them.

Above: *Rodeo* desk and chair, Garouste and Bonetti, 1990, produced in a limited edition for Neotu. Photograph by Karin Knoblich.

Opposite: *Berger* chair, Garouste and Bonetti, 1991, produced in a limited edition for Neotu. Photograph by Karin Knoblich.

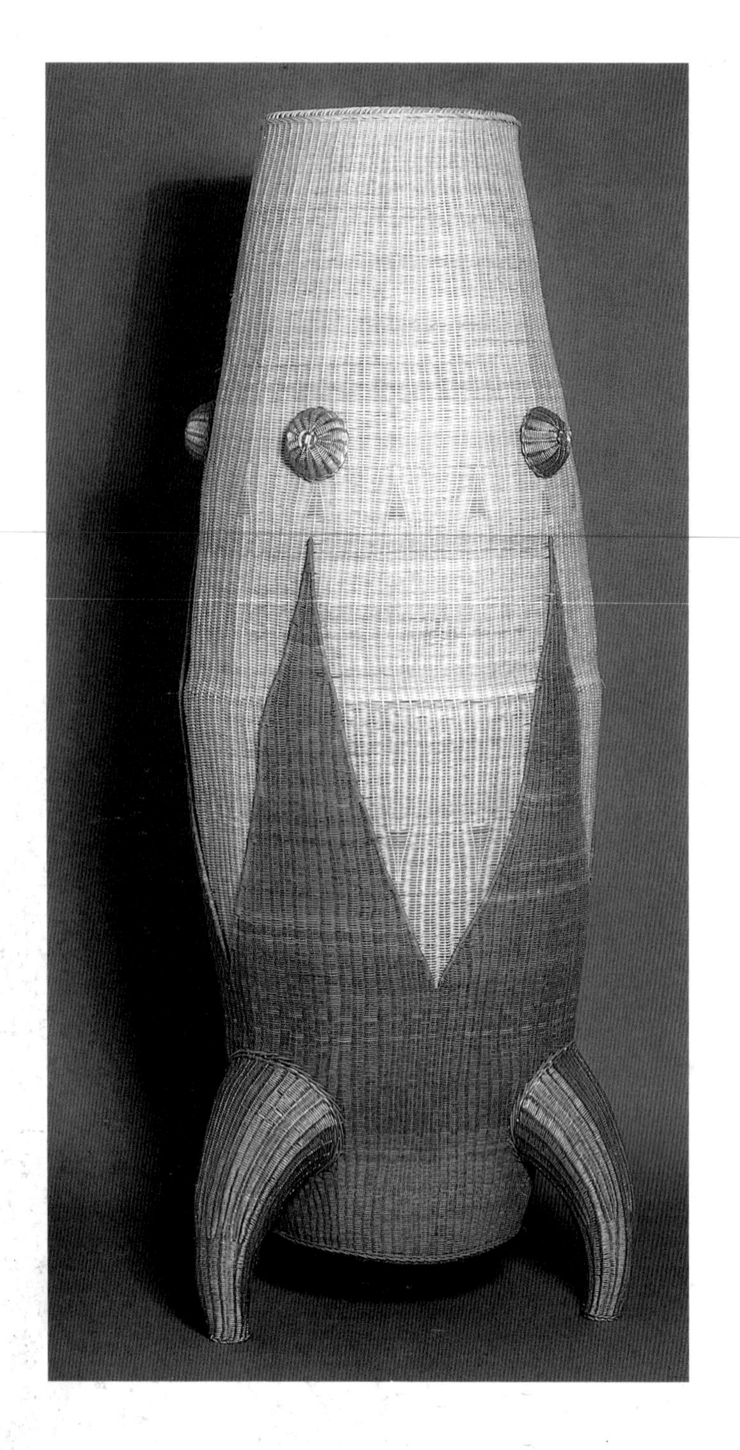

Left: *Tam Tam* lamp, Garouste and Bonetti, 1989, produced in a limited edition for Neotu. Photograph by Karin Knoblich.

Below: *Bronze* table, Garouste and Bonetti, 1986, produced in a limited edition by Neotu. Photograph courtesy of Neotu.

Opposite: *Music Cabinet*, Garouste and Bonetti, 1990, produced in a limited edition for Neotu. Photograph by Karin Knoblich.

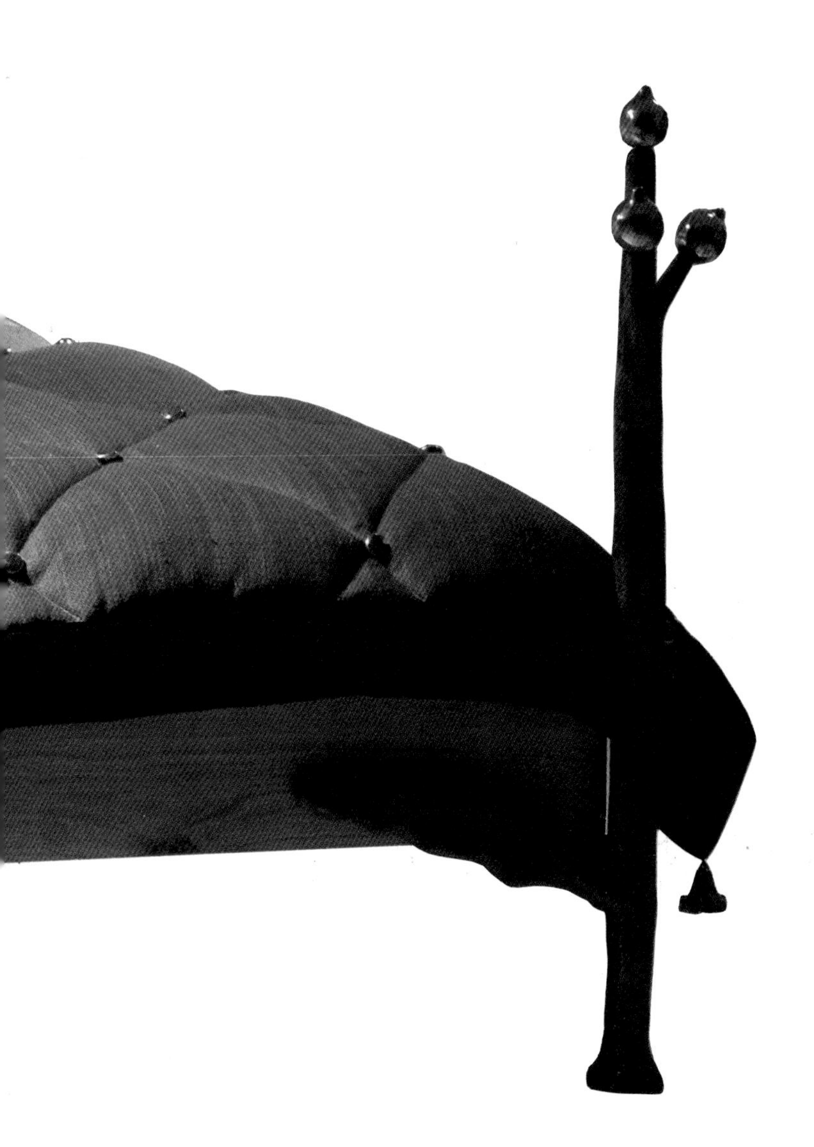

Above: *Afrika* table, Garouste and Bonetti, 1990, produced in a limited edition for Neotu. Photograph by Karin Knoblich.

Left: *Beau Rêve* (beautiful dream) bed, Garouste and Bonetti, 1990, produced in a limited edition for Neotu. Photograph by Karin Knoblich.

The Primitive movement found a permanent home in the Paris gallery En Attendant les Barbares (Waiting for the Barbarians), where its directors Frederic De Luca and Agnès Bellebeau have assembled the work of modern barbarians including Garouste and Bonetti, Cherif Medjeber, and Migeon and Migeon. De Luca started his gallery at a time when Philippe Starck was conquering the design world via Japan, New York, and Italy. Unquestionably, Starck had taken French design out of oblivion while taking design in general into more media-oriented times. But, even with Starck's success and with the work of the generation of designers he continues to inspire, De Luca and his artists felt that there was something missing, something left unexpressed. That "something" is now represented in the work of several artists whose medium is furniture and whose spirit is that of explorers seeking a new history. They are searching to find new forms, materials, and, in fact, new languages with which to create animated objects. From the gallery to the home, the idea is to create a mix of beautiful objects within a poetic space, a space that reflects the individual and, in many ways, reflects the New Age mentality of the 1990s. The search for expression of the inner self and self-determination, by way of nature, crystals, and tranquilizing music, parallels a desire for furniture with a tactile, primitive spirit. The effect of these new interiors, says De Luca, "is very modern, [but] less aggressive, less industrial." The buyer is investing in function but also in a bit of the spiritual, something that pleases and gives one much the same pleasure as buying art.

Right: Chest of drawers, Garouste and Bonetti, 1989, produced in a limited edition for En Attendant les Barbares. Photograph courtesy of En Attendant les Barbares.

Opposite: Tripod floor lamp, cage, and chair from the *Barbarian* collection, Garouste and Bonetti, 1981, produced in a limited edition by Neotu. Photograph courtesy of Neotu.

Left: *Mask* lamp, Garouste and Bonetti, 1984, produced in a limited edition for En Attendant les Barbares. Photograph courtesy of En Attendant les Barbares.

Below: *Lune* (moon) lamp, Garouste and Bonetti, 1984, produced in a limited edition by En Attendant les Barbares. Photograph courtesy of En Attendant les Barbares.

For many a modern twentieth-century urbanite, the idea of a primitive interior is likely to bring to mind images of Barbarella and Fred Flintstone. The candlesticks and *Nomade* lamp of Migeon and Migeon seem just so inspired. Their unified forms, in animated primary colors or monochromatics, cannot escape a certain urban savvy, albeit mixed with a considerable amount of humor. For their *Troglodyte* collection, Migeon and Migeon went further back, not in time, but within the history of their own work and recollections to create forms devoid of preconceived notions. Trying to start at a personal ground zero, they left out the color and worked within the properties of the material, a synthetic resin, from liquid to solid, concentrating on form and texture. Form, in each of their designs, is in a state of evolution, breaking out of rock or seemingly eaten through by sandstorms. The objects are finished at the point of transformation, but it has been a slow, quiet journey. Migeon and Migeon do not consider themselves spontaneous in their actions. They ponder the possibilities in design, enjoying the mix of elements, allowing what will be to be.

Below: *AH* and *OH* tables, Migeon and Migeon, 1990, produced in a limited edition for Artistes and Modeles. Photograph by Dominique Feintrenie.

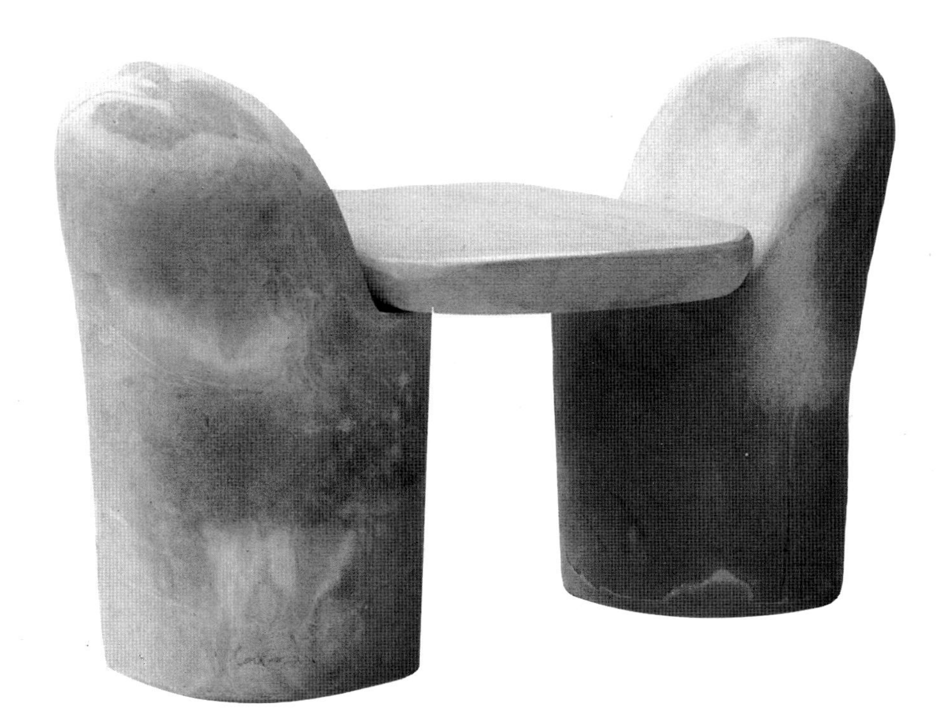

Above: Covered box, lamp, and candlesticks from the *Troglodyte* collection, Migeon and Migeon, 1990, produced in a limited edition by the artists for En Attendant les Barbares. Photograph courtesy of En Attendant les Barbares.

Left: *Ararat* stool, Migeon and Migeon, 1990, produced in a limited edition by the artists for En Attendant les Barbares. Photograph courtesy of En Attendant les Barbares.

Opposite: *Yemen* console, Migeon and Migeon, 1990, produced in a limited edition for En Attendant les Barbares. Photograph courtesy of En Attendant les Barbares.

Opposite: Candlesticks, Migeon and Migeon, 1989, produced for En Attendant les Barbares. Photograph courtesy of En Attendant les Barbares.

Right: *Nomade* lamp, Migeon and Migeon, 1990, produced in a limited edition for Artistes and Modeles. Photograph by Dominique Feintrenie.

Also of the En Attendant les Barbares clan is Eric Schmitt. Schmitt, as so many of the young generation of French designers, has had no formal design training. His background includes composing music and sculpting. In the late 1980s, Schmitt began creating furniture and decorative objects of forged, twisted iron; here, at the forge, he continues to work. His slightly skewed and seemingly misproportioned designs bear the physical imprint of their maker in each bend, each solder. The importance of touch in his designs marks Schmitt as a Primitive designer. Primitive, not because his work recalls a preindustrialized time, but because it speaks of its unique maker. One of his best known designs is the *Orthodox* chair. The *Orthodox* prototype was created at Schmitt's forge, and the finished version produced by XO (whose creative director is Philippe Starck). This chair, despite its refinement and ability to be mass-produced, is still human and animated, ready to walk away on its elfin feet. With his 1991 collection for Neotu, Schmitt showed a growing mastery of the iron and a mature, clear voice of his own, which relied less on the decorative and more on the investigation of iron as a giver of form in a large-scale furniture collection.

Left: *Sellette* forged-iron table with bronze details, Eric Schmitt, 1991, produced in a limited edition for Neotu. Photograph courtesy of Neotu.

Opposite: Chairs, Eric Schmitt, 1990, produced in a limited edition for En Attendant les Barbares. Photograph courtesy of En Attendant les Barbares.

Left: *Gueridon* table, Eric Schmitt, 1991, produced in a limited edition for Neotu. Photograph courtesy of Neotu.

Below: Forged-iron table, Eric Schmitt, 1991, produced in a limited edition for Neotu. Photograph courtesy of Neotu.

Opposite: Forged-iron chair, Eric Schmitt, 1991, produced in a limited edition for Neotu. Photograph courtesy of Neotu.

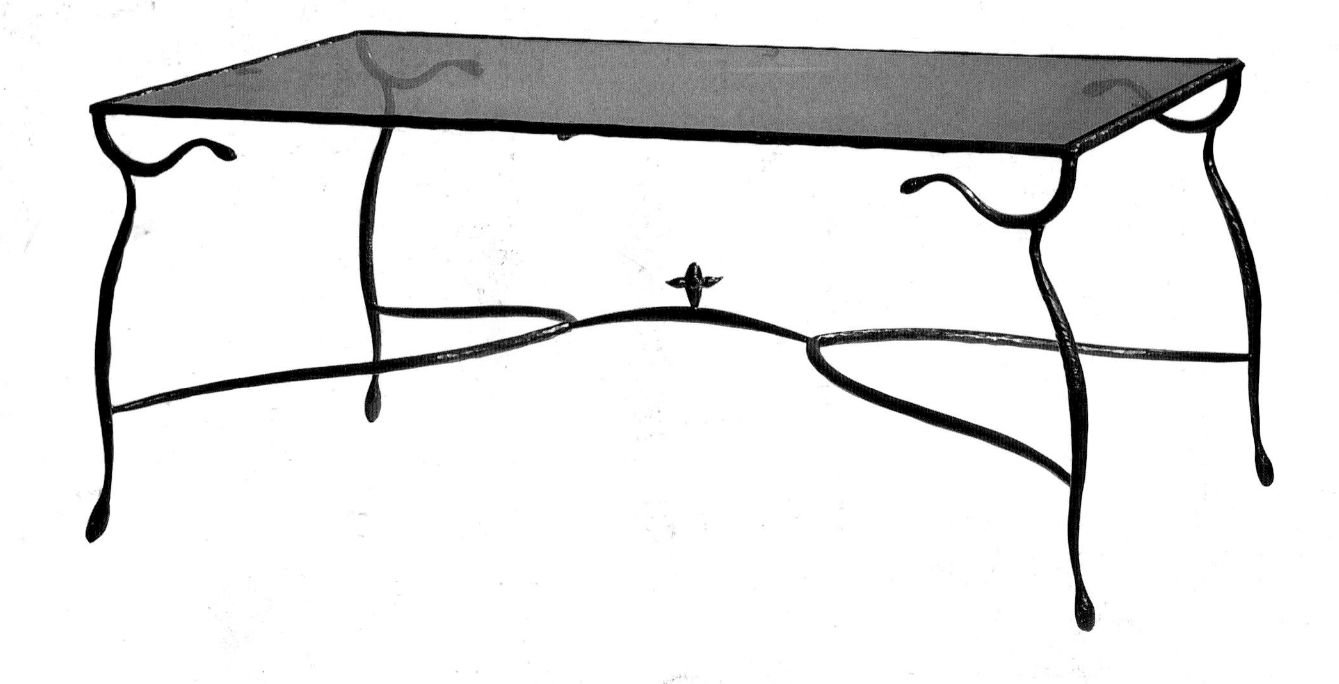

Right: Forged-iron table, Eric Schmitt, 1990, produced in a limited edition for En Attendant les Barbares. Photograph courtesy of En Attendant les Barbares.

Below: *Marie Antoinette* table, Eric Schmitt, 1989, produced in a limited edition by the artist for En Attendant les Barbares. Photograph courtesy of En Attendant les Barbares.

Opposite: *Orthodox* chairs, Eric Schmitt, 1989, produced by XO. Photograph courtesy of XO.

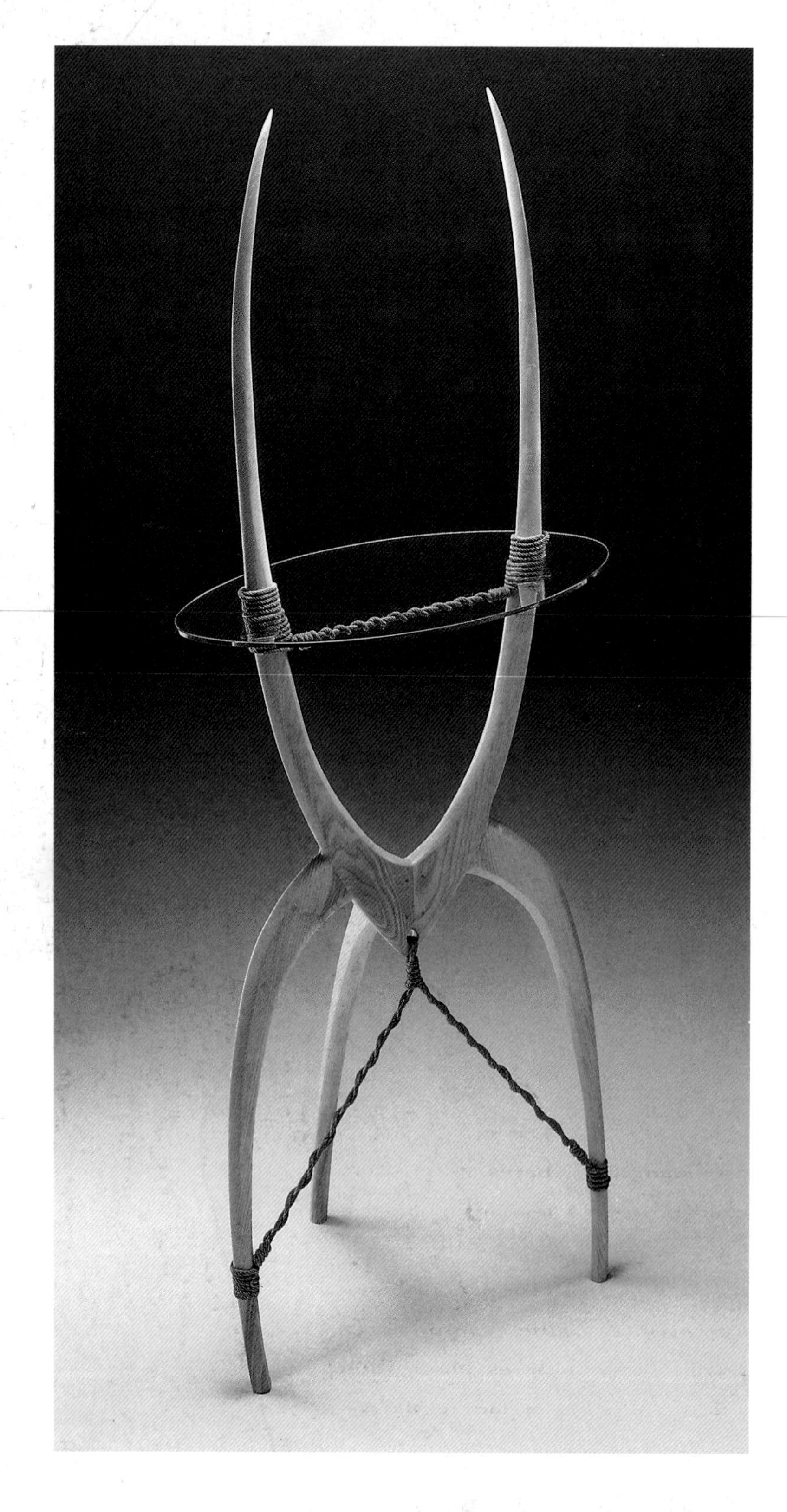

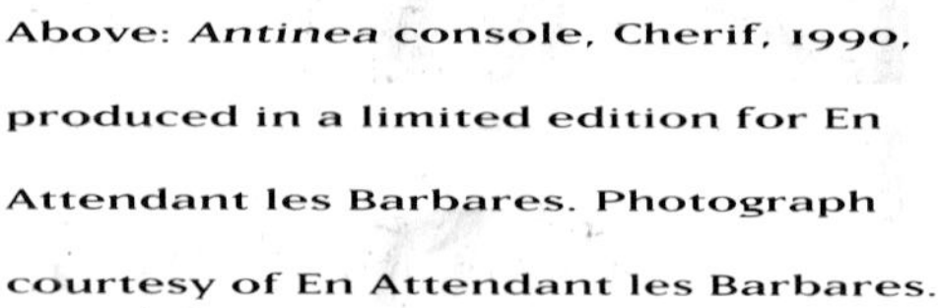

Above: *Antinea* console, Cherif, 1990, produced in a limited edition for En Attendant les Barbares. Photograph courtesy of En Attendant les Barbares.

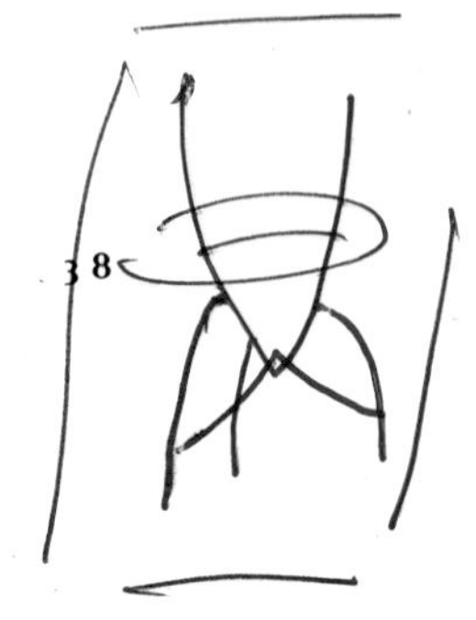

At the arrival of the twenty-first century, Primitivism is staking a claim for the future of the individual. The individual is represented in the user, someone who seeks to reinhabit the environment, and in the maker, whose ideas, mark, and name are embedded in his creation. In many instances, Primitivism is influenced by African and Arab art. These cultures are introducing a new vitality and sensuality into European design. Arab designers such as Yamo and Cherif, both living and working in France today, have brought sinewy forms, rattan, cord, and ethnicity to Europe. More important, however, they have opened European design to a pluralism, which realistically mirrors the makeup of its people.

Cherif Medjeber does not define himself solely as an Arab designer. Indeed, his work has universal, human appeal. Cherif moved to Paris in 1985 from his native Algeria. Although he had studied architecture in Tunis, architecture proved to be a medium that frustrated the directions in which his ideas were taking him; as often happens, certain periods of architectural study, dominated by doctrines considered correct at that moment, limit the students who do not fit in (an experience more in the vein of Howard Roark's than Le Corbusier's). Cherif created over sixty ceramic frescoes around Algiers, and became the amateur boxing champion of Algeria in the heavyweight division. He eventually found the means to express his personal and cultural vision through furniture design. He studied at L'Ecole Supérieure des Arts Décoratifs in Paris, the same school where Jean-Claude Maugirard of VIA, Philippe Starck, and others have guided a generation of designers who conform to no single design doctrine.

Cherif's work is his passion. The taut wooden shapes seem at once unapproachable and instinctively familiar. How does one sit on the stool? Does one sit at all, or is it sculpture? These are questions often asked of Cherif by a public that lacks the natural sensuality still appreciated in non-Western societies. His forms resemble prehistoric carvings of animals, but are more graceful. A gazelle balances a glass table top on its back. Two antlers piercing another glass table are captured in twisted cord. A light shines through an ancient animal skull from the floor of a river bed. For an artist just

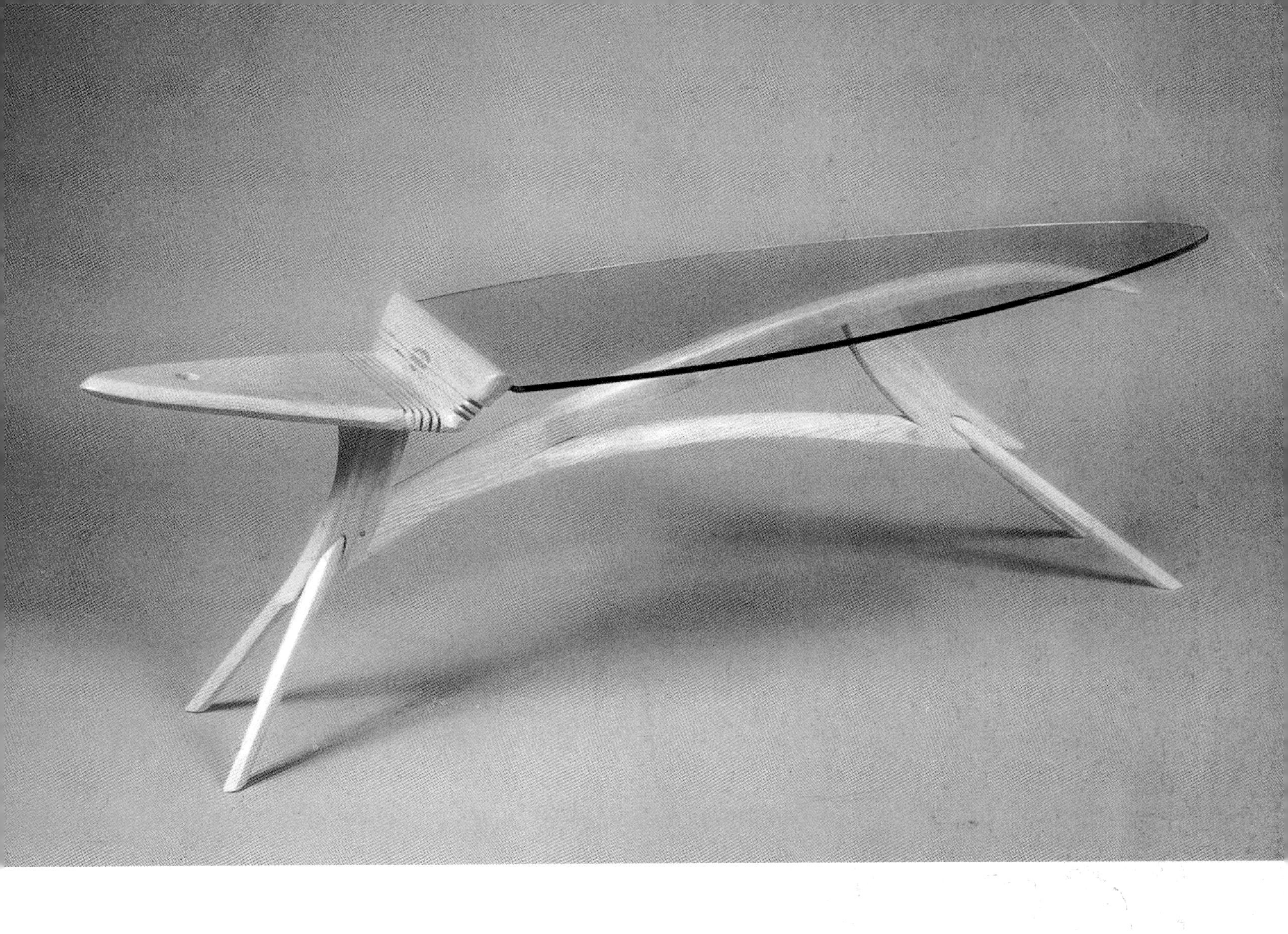

reaching thirty, the years of searching already seem far behind. Each piece exhibits an originality that is like a breath of fresh air in the often staid world of European design. So, yes, take it home and definitely use it as furniture and know that without these objects your rooms would never have the same presence.

Above: Glass-topped table, Cherif, 1990, produced in a limited edition for En Attendant les Barbarès. Photograph courtesy of En Attendant les Barbares.

Below: Bench and stool, Cherif, 1990, produced in a limited edition for En Attendant les Barbares. Photograph courtesy of En Attendant les Barbares.

Opposite: *C 17* chair, Yamo, 1990, prototype produced with an endowment from VIA. Photograph courtesy of VIA.

Right: Salt and pepper shakers, Yamo, 1990, produced by Techniland. Photograph courtesy of Techniland.

Below: *Altaïr* lamp, Cherif, 1991, produced by Techniland. Photograph courtesy of Techniland.

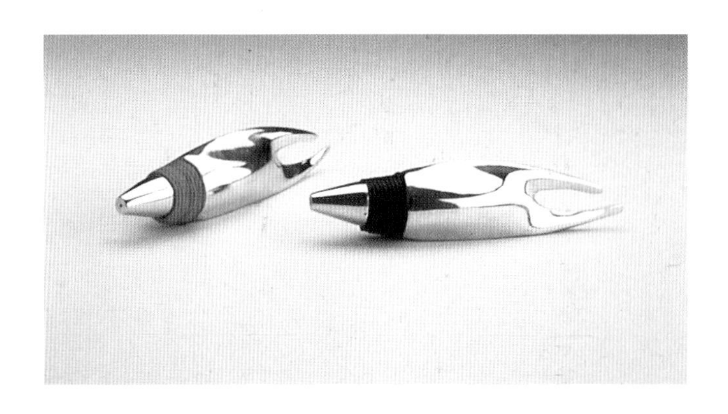

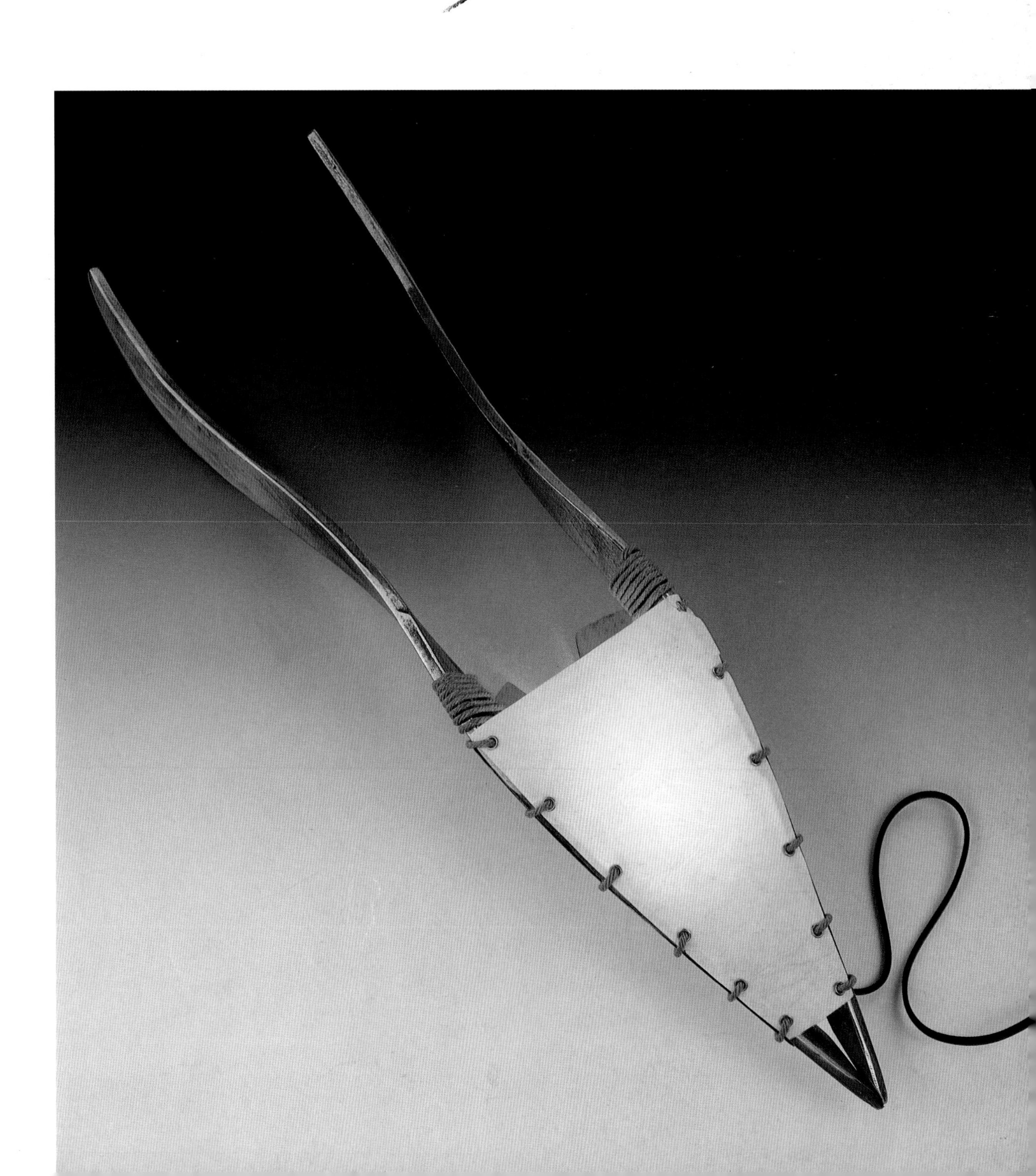

Olivier Gagnère's designs for furniture, glass, and terra-cotta objects have come to define the essence of the Primitive spirit: the concept of the perfected imperfection. So much of his work—the forms, the details—seems to arise out of a personal well of childlike and utopian inspirations. Gagnère has had no academic design training. He has followed his own personal discoveries as an artist and has collaborated with designers such as Ettore Sottsass. He is impassioned with the exploration and mastery of a variety of crafts, which is a necessity since his work, though primitive in spirit, is complex to produce. He begins by drawing a finished image and then sets out to make the piece exactly in those materials he conceived. For Gagnère, each new idea is a process of rediscovery, working with master craftsmen, merging a perfectionism with a Primitive *joie de vivre.*

Opposite: Terra-cotta vase, Olivier Gagnère, 1989, produced in a limited edition for Galerie Adrien Maeght. Photograph courtesy of Galerie Adrien Maeght.

Above: Vase, Olivier Gagnère, 1988, produced in a limited edition for Galerie Adrien Maeght. Photograph by Gilles Voisin.

Left: Murano glass bowl, Olivier Gagnère, 1988, produced in a limited edition for Galerie Adrien Maeght. Photograph courtesy of Galerie Adrien Maeght.

Below: Oak folding screen with gold-leaf motifs (detail), Olivier Gagnère, 1990, manufactured by Fourniture. Photograph courtesy of Galerie Adrien Maeght.

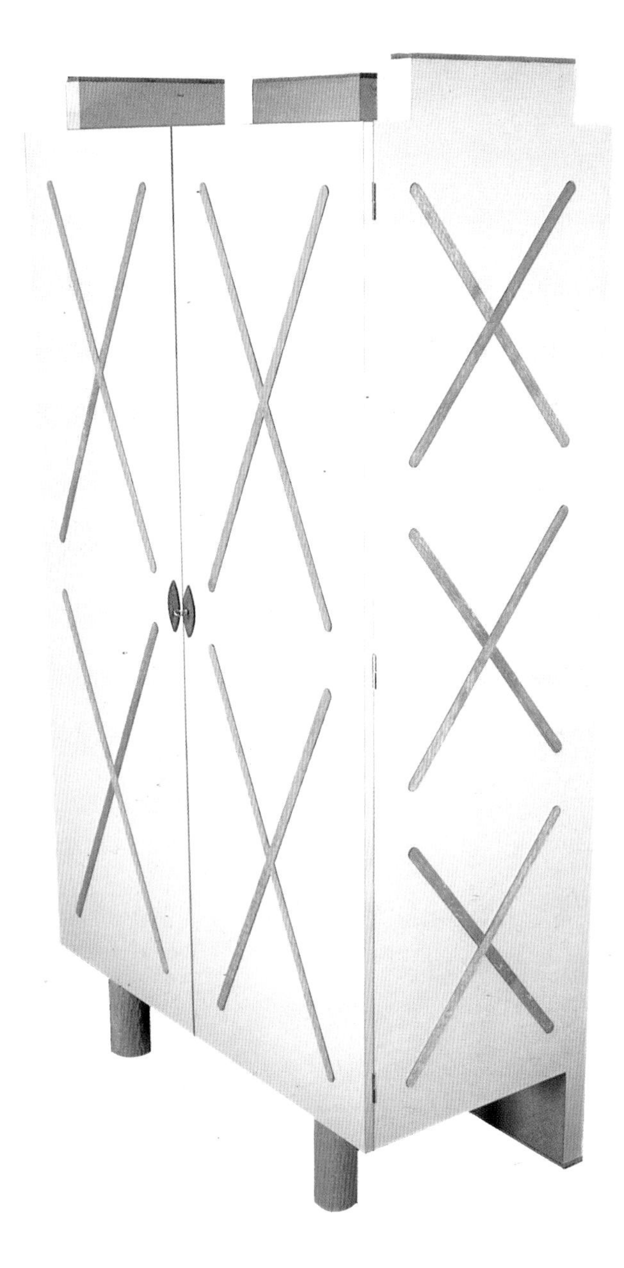

Left: Armoire, Olivier Gagnère, 1990, manufactured by Fourniture. Photograph courtesy of Galerie Adrien Maeght.

Below: Carpet, Olivier Gagnère, 1990, produced in a limited edition for Galerie Yves Gastou. Photograph courtesy of Galerie Yves Gastou.

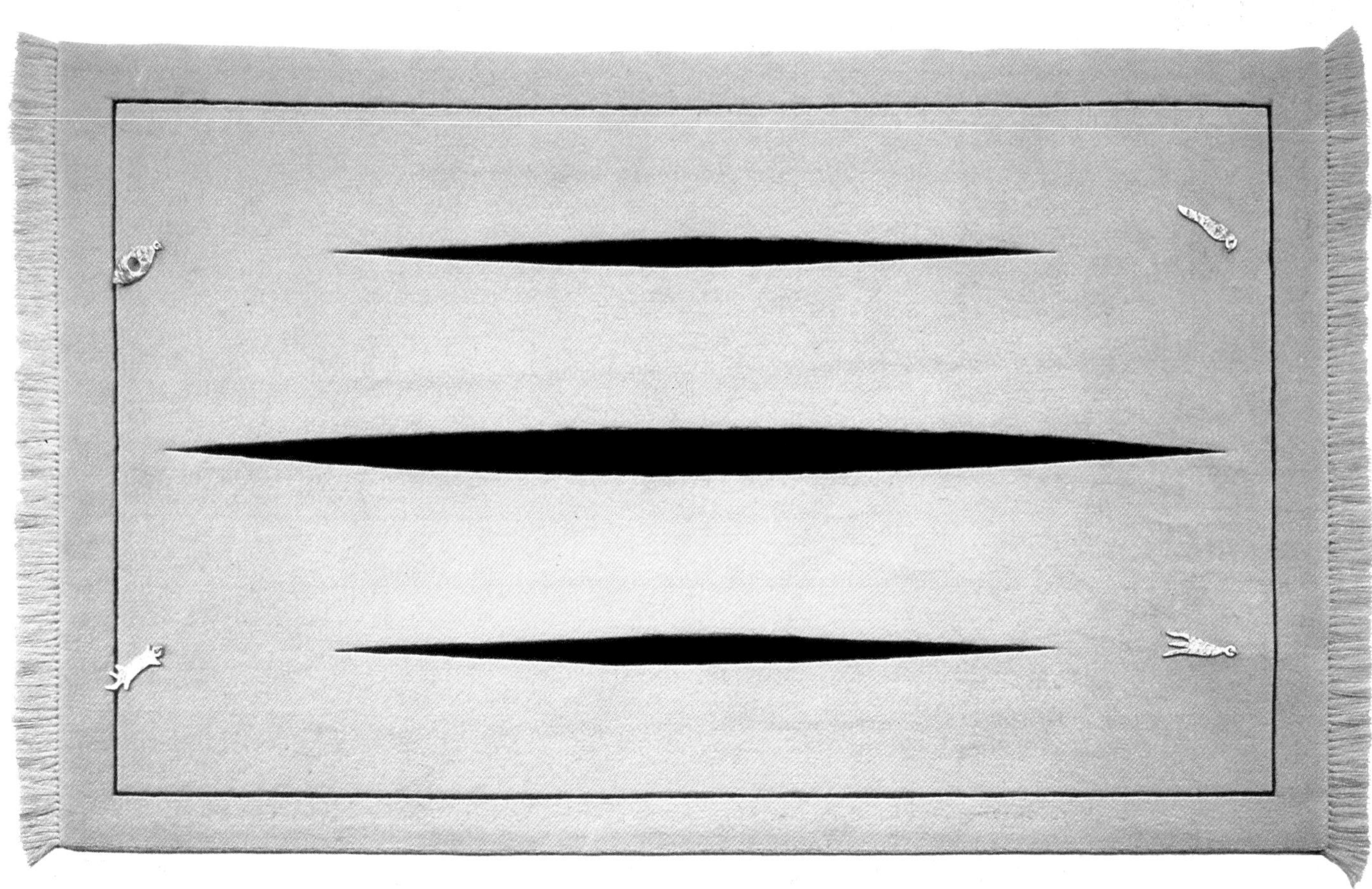

Primitivism is in the gesture, the person, not in the means of execution. The means can involve all that technology has to offer and all that has always been, the best of the artisan's knowledge and trade; for example, Gagnère's glass vases seem impossible at first glance to have been realized. The milky white vases, at once opaque and translucent, are made of two layers of glass. The colored pieces of glass are fused to the vase solely with heat. The cooling of different colors of glass at different temperatures makes each creation an exacting exercise. For the production of many of the pieces, Gagnère went to Venice to work with the expert craftsmen there because, he says, "they had the technique which was best for the design." Gagnère continually seeks to "encounter the technique," wherever it may take him. He has opened the world of decorative objects to the same freedoms other artists enjoy, as close to the mode of spontaneous creation as a craftsman's hands will allow.

Gagnère's collection for Fourniture contains the same mix of precision and primitive imagery. The unmistakable Gagnère signs are all present: the X motif, the mix of materials from gauged oak to slate and gold leaf, the exacting joining of different elements, and, finally, the mischievous figures like those that appear on his folding screen. The Fourniture collection is far more readily producible than the glass objects; wood, of course, is more pliable and, just as important, Fourniture is committed to join the creators with the expertise and understanding of its craftsmen and to make the work available to the public. There is no loss of the Primitive qualities in the production. The heavy table legs and the innate sense of decoration which has no predecessor are all preserved.

Opposite: Table, Olivier Gagnère, 1988, produced in a limited edition for Galerie Adrien Maeght. Photograph courtesy of Galerie Adrien Maeght.

Below: Oak table with felt-covered legs, Olivier Gagnère, 1990, manufactured by Fourniture. Photograph courtesy of Galerie Adrien Maeght.

Opposite: Green and blue vase, Olivier Gagnère, 1988, produced in a limited edition for Galerie Adrien Maeght. Photograph courtesy of Galerie Adrien Maeght.

Gagnère has also worked in terra cotta, a material that tests the simplicity of his convictions. Being true to the material, Gagnère has created vases which seem the most primitive of his projects. They are somehow less concerned with proportion or elegance. Without the play of light which glass allows, or the assembly of different materials found in his furniture, the terra-cotta pieces are strictly about form and its balance with the material. The knobby detailing grows from the base, as if the artist's fingers are still working, pushing the material. Gagnère's goal is to create an object with a simplicity that allows it to stand alone. Simplicity in form, however, is not necessarily in opposition to complexity in production.

Gagnère does not seek to be difficult; he seeks to work with the greatest richness allowable in the collaboration with the artisan, a collaboration which offers the artist the means to explore and to produce things more quickly than would be the case going through the ranks of a large manufacturer. "It is only recently," says Gagnère, "that the means have become available for the artists to create objects with the large producers, and only because they too have grasped the desire of the public, in this epoch, to possess and cultivate the object." Gagnère sees this period in our culture as one in which our sensibility for the object as it enriches our habitat is on a level with our rapport with music or art. Whether this phenomenon lasts is not important. What is important is to create objects that will be important in the future; the simple things usually endure. And, as Gagnère says, "things that are modern today are the things which are always modern." He believes in objects that will mix through the ages and retain their appeal. If Gagnère's objects stay in the memory, it is because they are charged with a simplicity that rests on an emotional level.

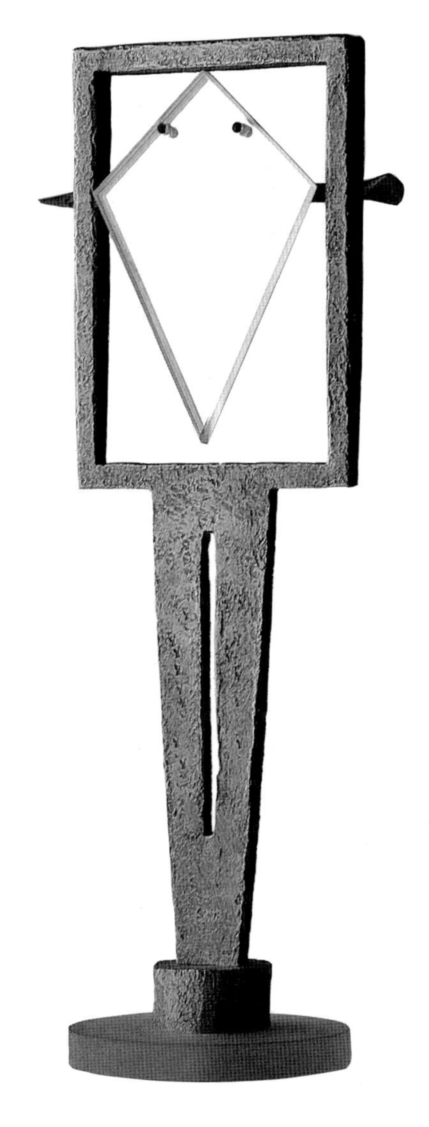

Left: *Barbière* mirror, Olivier Gagnère, 1987, produced in a limited edition for Galerie Adrien Maeght. Photograph courtesy of Galerie Adrien Maeght.

Below left: Bronze and glass candelabra, Olivier Gagnère, 1988, produced in a limited edition for Galerie Adrien Maeght. Photograph courtesy of Galerie Adrien Maeght.

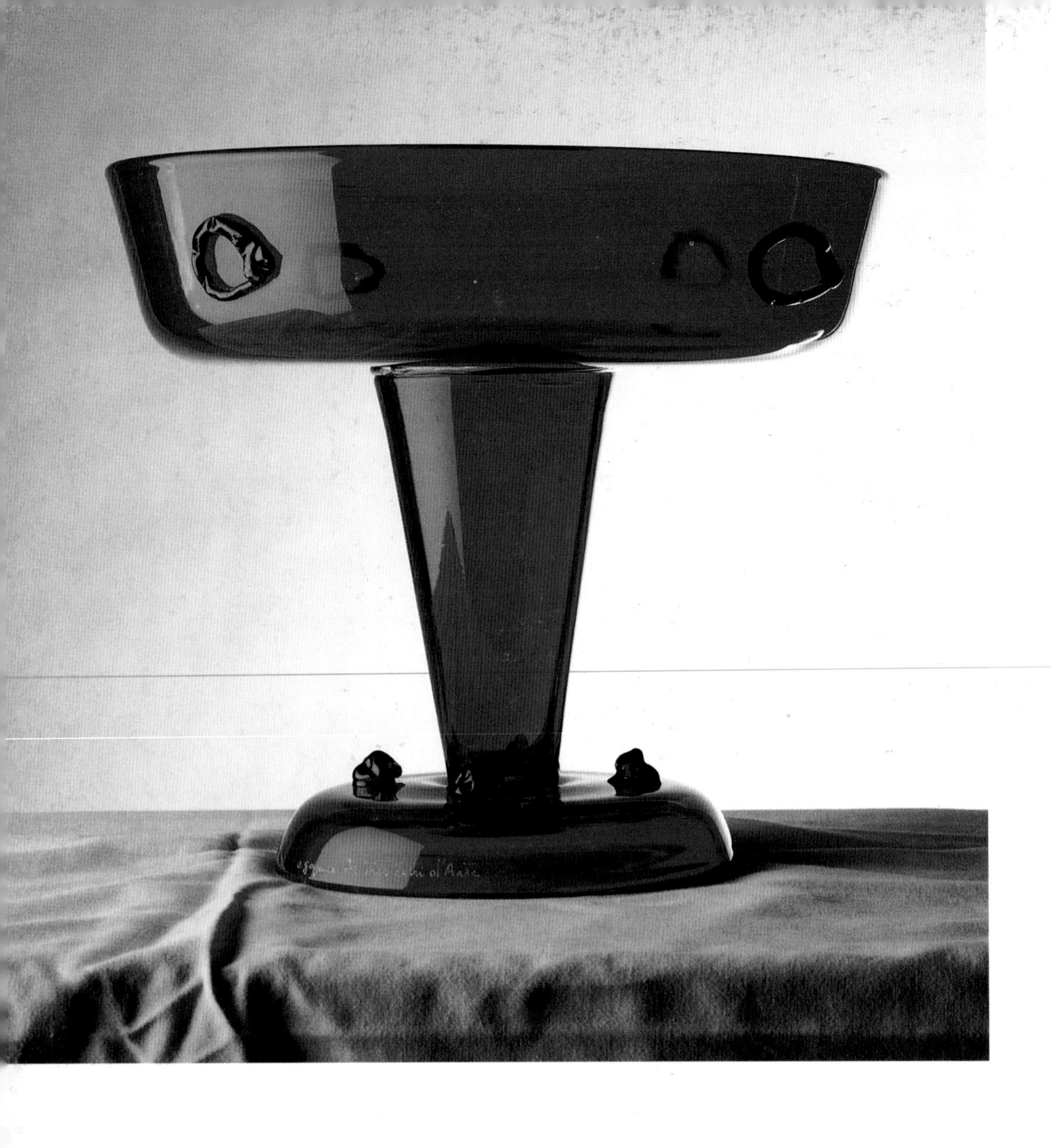

Left: Red and blue Murano glass bowl, Olivier Gagnère, 1988, produced in a limited edition for Galerie Adrien Maeght. Photograph courtesy of Galerie Adrien Maeght.

Below: Collection of Quimper ceramics, Olivier Gagnère, 1991. Photograph by Pascal Lachaume, courtesy of Galerie Adrien Maeght.

Above: Vase (detail), Christian Astuguevieille, 1990, produced in a limited edition by the artist. Photograph by Laziz Hamani.

Below: Cord totem, Christian Astuguevieille, 1989, produced in a limited edition by the artist. Photograph by Laziz Hamani.

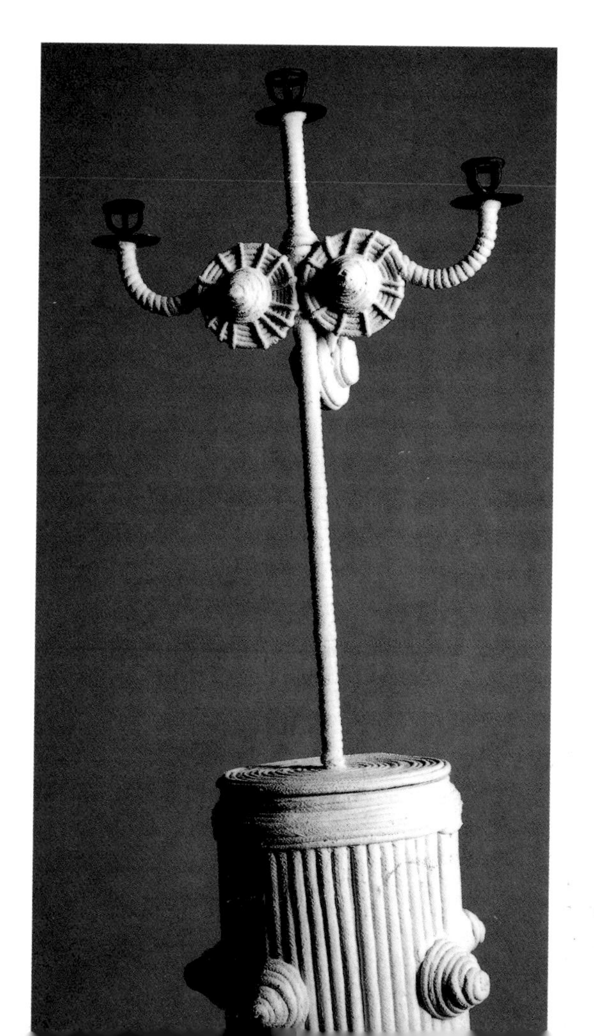

Because of his love for the touch of objects and for the sensuality of form and environment, Christian Astuguevieille creates first for the man of his imagination. He bases each collection on an imagined scenario, complete with identifiable characters, which is recounted to us mortal men through the tactility of the material, most often cord. His imagination has taken him, for example, to the hunter, a hero for whom he created the necessary, or perhaps unnecessary, objects for his daily living, his pageants, and his mysteries. Astuguevieille has recently moved towards creating for the man of the real world, concentrating, however, on totems. With so many things already created for utilitarian needs, Astuguevieille provides the objects of celebration for his everyday heroes. His ideas are utopian; he is a positive oracle in a cold world.

Astuguevieille has always been involved in increasing awareness of tactility and abstract ideas in art. Early in his career, he worked with children who had problems with elocution and instructed their teachers on developing techniques to reach them. For five years, he directed the children's studio/gallery at the Centre Georges Pompidou in Paris, working with ideas of tactility and the comprehension of space. His design work during this period began with jewelry launched in his Paris boutique and used extensively in the Paris fashion shows; he also worked with the great perfume

houses, in researching forms for flacons and as creative director for Rochas. Bringing his energies to larger objects and furniture, Astuguevieille relied on all of his talents, creating objects with a story and a strong tactile image. He arrives at these images without drawings; he works with craftsmen by talking and describing as a storyteller, with physical gestures, his imagined object.

The furniture of Astuguevieille inhabits a space in an animated way. Each piece expresses emotion. For him, the greatest compliment is when he is told, "I have touched, and I understand." He is fascinated by the idea of the furniture actually rearranging the house, when the furniture or totems seem to move of their own accord until they have filled all corners of the house at one time or another. The primitive—in this case, tribal—inspirations in the furniture give each piece a life of its own.

Primitivism is instantly recognizable in design: it is human, poetic, and heroic. Primitivism is, however, difficult to define within a vocabulary formed through many formal, rational decades which have rendered the fictitious "impure," the craft "nonprogressive," and the emotive "decadent." These narrow concepts rapidly lose validity when confronted with the intelligence of designers such as Astuguevieille, Gagnère, or Garouste and Bonetti. Each has worked through ten or more years of design, experimenting and, indeed, existing in urban, designed environments. Primitivism today is a reaction against what has been overly processed. Primitivism is of the undictated, the rediscovered, and the untold story. One can easily imagine rising from the *Afrika* table, blowing out the candles held in the bronze and glass design of Olivier Gagnère, and then falling asleep in the *Beau Rêve* bed, content with the imaginative journey. Primitivism is the tactile and the comforting.

Left: Cord totem, Christian Astuguevieille, 1988, produced in a limited edition by the artist. Photograph by Laziz Hamani.

Opposite: Cord chair, Christian Astuguevielle, 1989, produced in a limited edition by the artist. Photograph by Laziz Hamani.

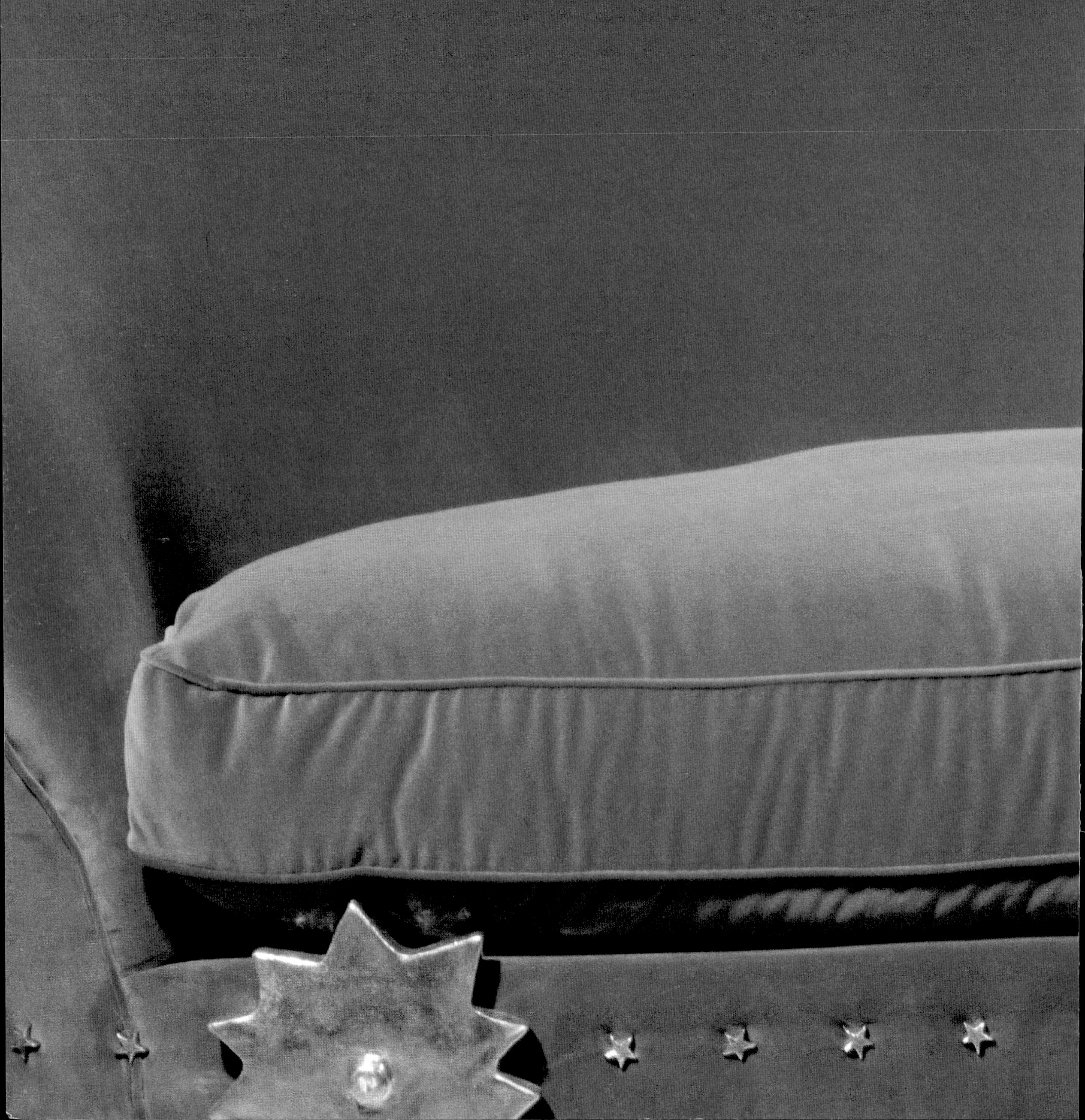

The New Baroque

The signs of the New Baroque—loss of symmetry, ingenuity of ornament, sensuality of movement—seem somehow too timely an occurrence to end a decadent and materialistic era. If our vocabulary and vision were to remain limited, the opulence could be quickly termed superficial, and the decorative detailing, dishonest. The New Baroque is the expression of spectacle. Its new energy goes beyond the veneer and includes a universality of form and image, which defies a single aesthetic. The New Baroque embraces invention, self-expression and indulgence.

The New Baroque is not directly based in theory or history. The masters of baroque, such as Borromini, were considered modernists in their time; the new adherents, too, look to the present for inspiration. Today, the present includes the past. A visit to a museum or to a video arcade can provide inspiration, possibly for the same design. So, as their predecessors were, the designers of the New Baroque will be accused of "capricious novelties."[6] Indeed, after many decades of sleek black forms defining a supposedly modern intellectual mode, a gold-leaf doorknob might seem capricious, yet can it be any less of our time?

The New Baroque is more than a change of outward appearance; it is a change of priorities. The narrative and the tactile have become more important than the purity of form and aesthetic distance. Here the New Baroque coincides with the definition of its predecessor: "The art of the Baroque concentrates on vivid images of situations, real and surreal, rather than on 'history' and absolute form."[7]

Along with powerful visuals, the New Baroque relies on a parallel text: a story central to its being. From the fiction the form arrives. The fiction builds the rapport between the object, the interior, and the user. The text, however, might not be found in the form of the written word, but in visual language. The New Baroque spirit is found in a Fellini film or a David Byrne music video. It seeks to tell the story in the language of the times.

The New Baroque confesses a relationship to fashion—to emotional indulgence and material cravings. It has affinities with the cult of the object pervading current culture, which has allowed furniture to be collected in the way that art and designer-label jackets are. The designers of the New Baroque are both artists and cultural critics. They are perhaps self-serving in their urge to create certain jewel-like pieces, without specific clients or markets in mind, but they are also wholly savvy to the timeliness of their creations in a world rushed with new stimuli.

Opposite: *Corbeille* sofa (detail), Garouste and Bonetti, 1990, produced in a limited edition for Neotu. Photograph by Karin Knoblich.

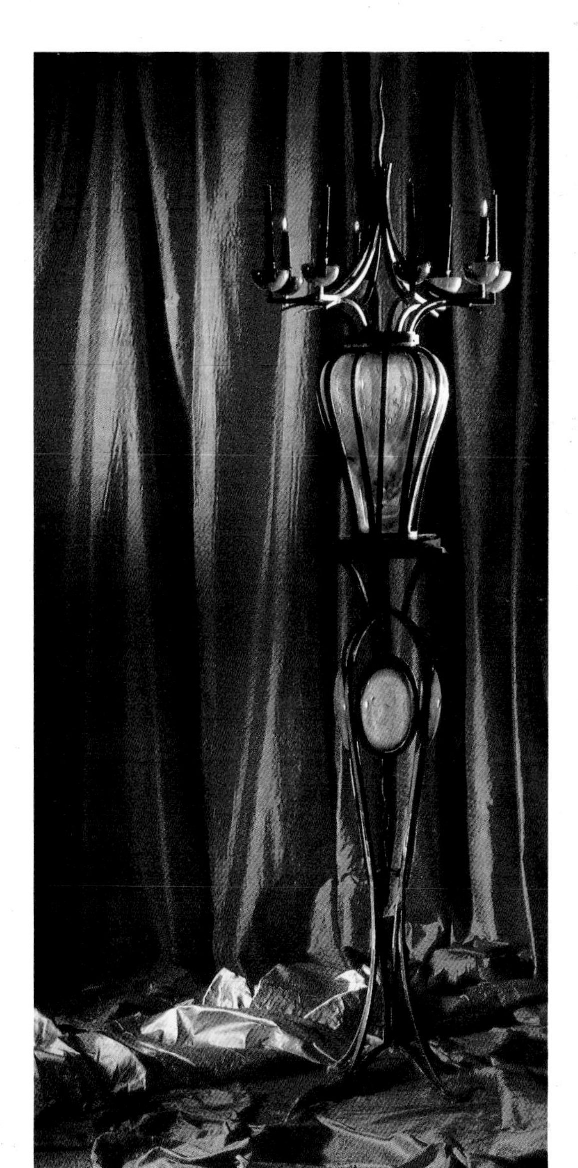

Left: *Shanghai* candelabra, André Dubreuil, 1990, produced in a limited edition by Daum. Photograph courtesy of Daum.

Left: *Paris* desk and chair, André Dubreuil, 1988, produced in a limited edition by the artist. Photograph by Edina van der Wyck.

Opposite: *Spine Chair*, André Dubreuil, 1989, produced in a limited edition by the artist. Photograph by Edina van der Wyck.

André Dubreuil was one of the first artists to gain notoriety for his New Baroque designs. Dubreuil creates exquisite, meticulously detailed furniture of hand-forged iron, gold, and copper. While Dubreuil's best-known design is the *Spine Chair*, a curving ladder of forged iron (one of the few pieces that his atelier has duplicated), his imprint is instantly recognizable in a console or a candelabra.

Dubreuil learned to solder metal from fellow artist and, at that time, fellow Londoner Tom Dixon. "The debut," he says, "was simple, I was still learning." Later, his work became more complex, at times mysterious, as he became a better craftsman and his own harshest critic. Starting with forged iron and working it into curves and naturalistic forms which he finds subdue the aggressiveness of the metal, Dubreuil is interested in stretching the limits of the material. He is increasingly adding other materials to the forged iron: copper, glass beads, enamel. He finds his motivation in the material, letting it suggest a form. The resulting pieces have an intensity, even perversion, in their devotion to the richness of detail and materials.

Dubreuil's work is an antithesis to what he describes as "kitchen furniture," with its poverty of design, which ends in serviceable, but uninspired, furniture. He sees contemporary furniture design as limited in its use of mass-produced materials. The public has become very weary of this limited sameness, and is increasingly reacting against the mentality of buying and throwing away, prevalent in the 1980s. There is a gap to be filled between the homogeneous and disposable, and the well-built, original, and artistic. For his part, Dubreuil is working for the individual. His work is expensive, generally one-of-a-kind, and bought much as one buys a piece of art.

The public's desire to own unique, designed objects has not escaped the notice of manufacturers. Many producers of furniture and decorative objects are looking to bring new life to their collections through the resurrection of the artist-artisan collaboration. It is not just a question, however, of producing something different, something sellable; the public has become too design-conscious for that. It is a question of understanding the New Baroque aspects of display and dandyism, which have brought color, luxury materials, and—most important—artists to the design forefront. The New Baroque object is one to be shown off. It is the highlight of a period of decorative rediscovery. Only in the 1980s did Memphis arrive from Italy with boldly patterned and colored designs, allowing design followers to take a step beyond the International Style. Before this, the idea of decoration had become bourgeois, almost tacky, and was certainly not for the purists of design.

Above: Copper and steel chest with glass beads, André Dubreuil, 1989, produced as a unique piece by the artist. Photograph by Edina van der Wyck.

Opposite: Etched copper and enamel chest, André Dubreuil, 1990, produced as a unique piece by the artist. Photograph by Richard Burbridge.

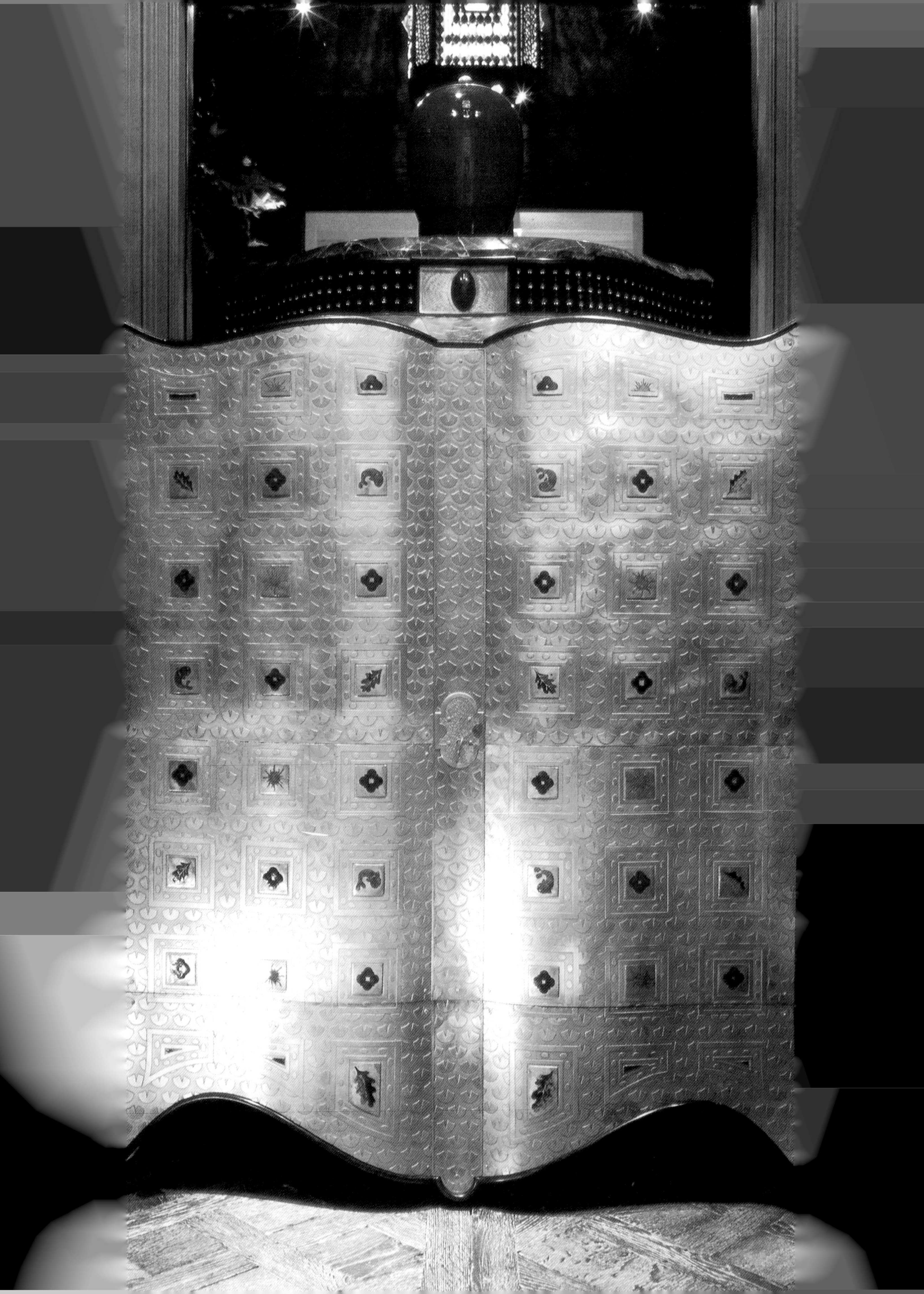

Left: Chest with cloisonné, André Dubreuil, 1991, produced as a unique piece by the artist. Photograph by Michael Amet.

Below: Carpet (detail), André Dubreuil, 1990, produced in a limited series by Galerie Yves Gastou. Photograph courtesy of Galerie Yves Gastou.

Opposite: Chair and cabinet, André Dubreuil, 1989, produced as unique pieces by the artist. Photograph courtesy of Galerie Gladys Mougin.

Above: Console, André Dubreuil, 1990, produced as a unique piece by the artist. Photograph courtesy of Galerie Gladys Mougin.

Opposite: Console, clock, and mirror, André Dubreuil, 1990, produced as unique pieces by the artist. Photograph courtesy of Galerie Gladys Mougin.

Reintroducing the designer to the manufacturer has resulted in many productive collaborations. André Dubreuil was invited by Daum, the century-old French crystal manufacturer, to create new designs in crystal and forged iron. In the rejuvenation that has taken place at Daum, artists, including Philippe Starck, Garouste and Bonetti, and Hilton McConnico, have designed collections under the direction of Clotilde Bacri. They were invited to work with the Daum master craftsmen and to choose the techniques that would best suit their designs. Starck chose the technique of mouth-blown glass of the 1950s, while Garouste and Bonetti worked with *pâte de verre,* a sculpted glass technique by which broken colored crystals are poured into molds creating opaque forms. Dubreuil was inspired by the work of Majorelle, done in the 1920s for Daum, an influence evident in his choice of colors that seem continually fluid within their iron cages. Daum intentionally chose artists who had little or no experience working with glass to form a collaboration that gives new meaning to the idea of decorative arts.

Collaboration with master craftsmen opens a vast resource for furniture designers, who less than ever are prisoners of a drawing board and who, after gaining the title "designer," are not likely to return to artisan status. Both Czech designer Borek Sípek and French designer Sylvain Dubuisson have been invited to work in porcelain at Sèvres. Dubuisson, noted for his award-winning light designs, has created a leaning Tower of Babel for Sèvres; Sípek, a setting of white day porcelain with lacy-cut edges and handles. The New Baroque would never have found its voice without the interest of the manufacturing houses, nor would these houses have become involved in high design without a generation of designers sympathetic to their aims and skills.

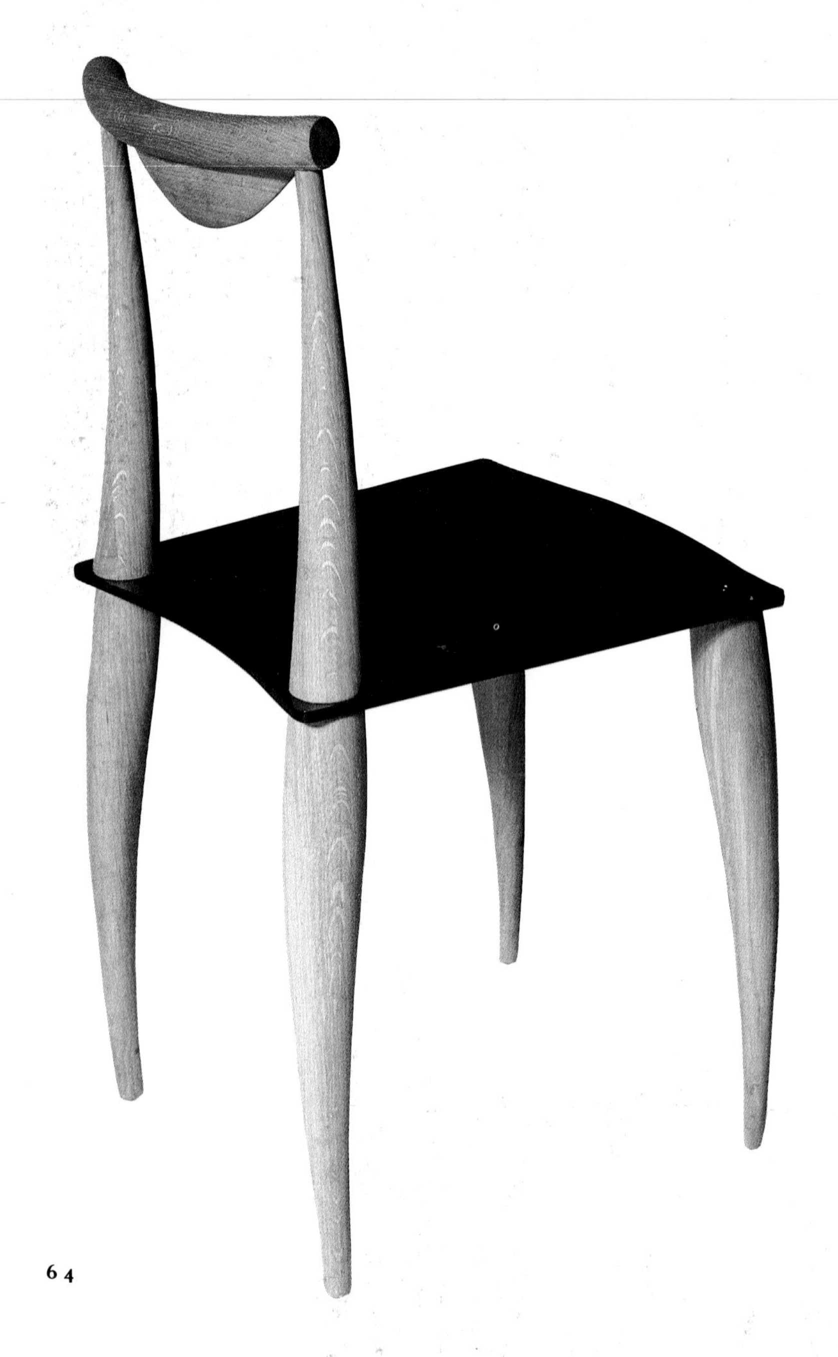

Left: *Bias* chair, Sylvain Dubuisson, 1990, manufactured by Fourniture. Photograph courtesy of VIA.

Right: Drawing of *Tower of Babel* lamp for Sèvres, Sylvain Dubuisson, 1990. Photograph courtesy of Sèvres.

Below: *4 Etrangetés sous un Mur* (four strange things under a wall) vase, Philippe Starck, 1988, produced in a limited edition by Daum. Photograph courtesy of Daum.

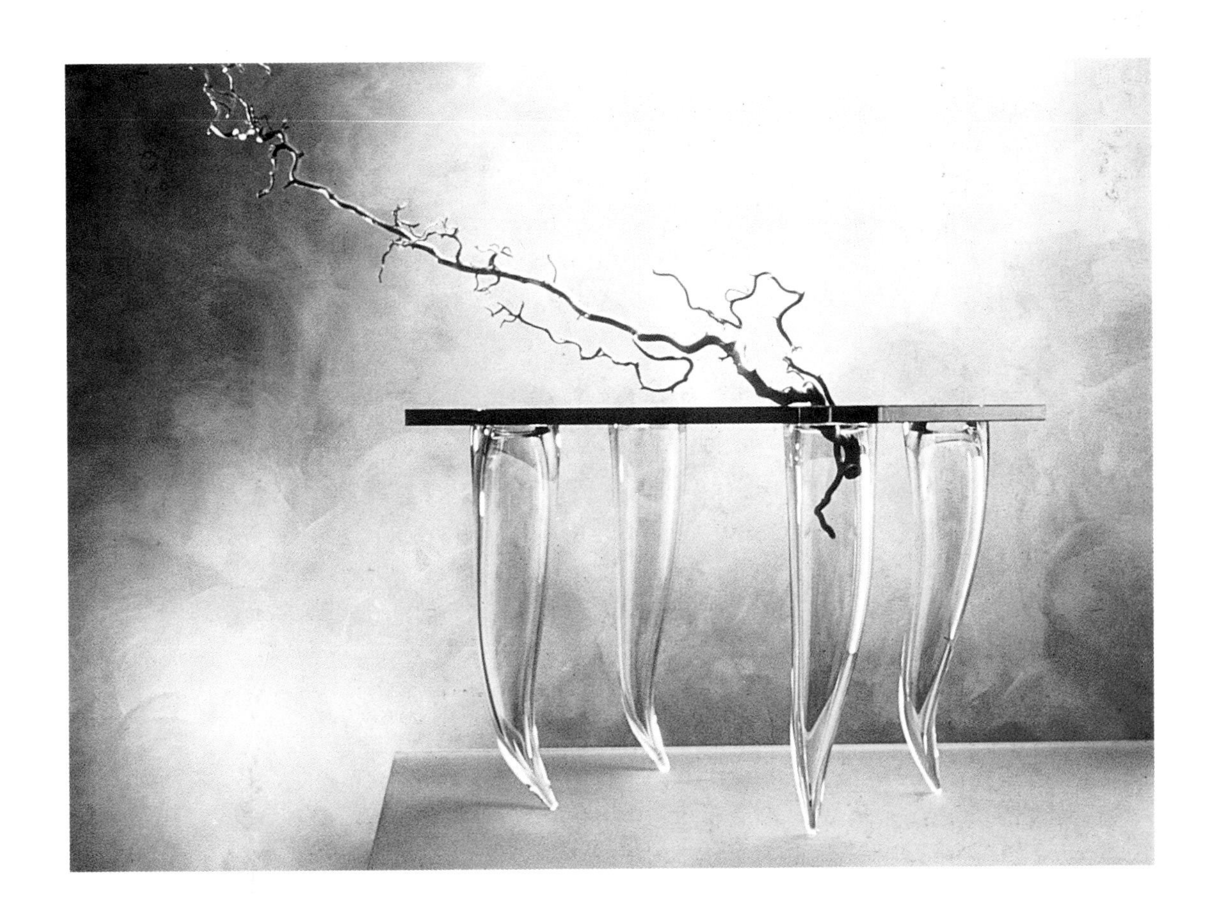

Above and Right: Ottoman and chair from the *Topkapi* collection with *Jalousie* carpet, Garouste and Bonetti, 1988, produced in a limited edition for En Attendant les Barbares. Photographs courtesy of En Attendant les Barbares.

Typical of the New Baroque designers who are working with several manufacturers and furniture galleries are Elizabeth Garouste and Mattia Bonetti. They have gone on to create whole interiors, which incorporate their furniture, objects, and whatever custom-designed fixtures are needed to create the desired mood. Their designs for Christian Lacroix's Paris boutique, for example, took the New Baroque beyond the realm of a few interesting pieces and into the field of viable interior solutions. At Lacroix, no element is left untouched by Garouste and Bonetti, including the flask for Lacroix's perfume, C'est La Vie. They have also, since their first interior collaboration on the restaurant Privilège at Paris's Palace discotheque, displayed the New Baroque tendency to integrate the various arts into their work. They worked with artist Gerard Garouste on the Privilège, incorporating elements of theater. They have a natural rapport with artists because they come from a diverse arts and design background themselves.

Like many leading designers of today, Garouste and Bonetti did not have a classic design-school-to-drawing-board experience. Elizabeth Garouste graduated from interior design school in the late 1970s and, finding little work available in her field, went on to work in fashion and set design. Mattia Bonetti, with a degree in textile design, worked as a fabric designer, an experience reflected in his watercolor sketches, his affinity to detail, and his inventive use of fabric and patterns. In addition, Bonetti designs jewelry. Working together, Garouste and Bonetti are at ease dreaming up beautiful pieces from a grab bag of ideas of which

Right and Below: Christian Lacroix Haute Couture Salon, Paris, furniture and interior design by Garouste and Bonetti, project begun in 1987. Photographs courtesy of Christian Lacroix.

the New Baroque is only one, though it is one in which they have excelled. If not consciously—they never chose to be "baroque"—they have captured the baroque sense of inventiveness and pageantry, creating modern spectacles, exactly the kind of places where haute couture dresses and princesses should be seen.

The project for the Princess and Prince Von Thurn und Taxis includes her private apartments and a restaurant for the museum at Regensburg Castle, for which they designed the furniture and cutlery. The restaurant addition was designed by German furniture designer and architect Volker Albus. (Albus has been a strong proponent of German design, designing, writing, and setting up exhibitions, notably "Capitales Europeénes du Nouveau Design.") With Garouste and Bonetti, Albus designed the scene for a Bavarian fantasy, in which the public dines as nobility. Now that Anthologie Quartett is producing the *Regensburg* chair, the fantasy can be experienced in the confines of any home.

Other Garouste and Bonetti collections could be termed New Baroque because of their incorporation of the ideals of pluralism, in which the celebration of the parts comes together to form a more vibrant whole. Other collections designed by Garouste and Bonetti include *Semainier* furniture, with colored glass inserts in starkly formed cabinets and tables, and the *Patchwork* collection, a study in skewed colored squares. *Patchwork* was the first collection for BGH, a company begun by Garouste and Bonetti to offer an easily produced and more affordable line of their designs. The form is a simple frame; twisted bronze details mark the corners, and patterns and emblems form the tableau. Each collection is based on a choice of fabric, used to cover lamps, or to slipcover chairs and tables. An embroidered flaming sun and a cloud-encircled moon are the thematic emblems of one collection, *Jour et Nuit* (Day and Night). Fabrics can be interchanged among collections. Is the use of the slipcover elevated to the level of chic, or is it simply make-do for those of us who want but cannot afford? It is hard to say whose side they are on. Garouste and Bonetti are always playing with the borders between the self-evident and illusion. They leave us to question their objectives. Are they *flaneurs* parading their finery for our snobbism or are they the mirror of our own daily posing?

Above: Slipcovered chairs from the *Jour et Nuit* (Day and Night) collection, Garouste and Bonetti, 1991, manufactured by BGH. Photograph courtesy of BGH.

Right: Champagne bucket, Garouste and Bonetti, 1990, produced in a limited edition for Neotu. Photograph by Karin Knoblich.

Opposite: Chair from the *Jour et Nuit* (Day and Night) collection, Garouste and Bonetti, 1988, produced in a limited edition for Neotu. Photograph by Karin Knoblich.

Left: *Palette* coffee table and rug from the *Patchwork* collection, Garouste and Bonetti, 1989, produced by BGH Editions. Photograph courtesy of VIA.

Below: *Corbeille* sofa, Garouste and Bonetti, 1990, produced in a limited edition for Neotu. Photograph by Karin Knoblich.

Opposite: *Gazebo* collection by Etamine with fabric designed by Garouste and Bonetti, 1990. Photograph courtesy of Etamine.

Above: *Jalousie* carpet (detail), Garouste and Bonetti, 1989, produced in a limited edition for En Attendant les Barbares. Photograph courtesy of En Attendant les Barbares.

Above right: *Cathedral* cabinet, Garouste and Bonetti, 1988, produced for Neotu. Photograph by Karin Knoblich.

Opposite: *Semainier* table, Garouste and Bonetti, 1988, produced in a limited edition for Neotu. Photograph courtesy of Neotu.

Above, top: *Tatlin* sofa, Roberto Semprini and Mario Cananzi, 1989, manufactured by Edra. Photograph courtesy of Edra.

Above, bottom: *Chamaleon* table and stool, Terry Pecora, 1991, manufactured by Edra. Photograph courtesy of Edra.

Covering up is a theme in much New Baroque furniture. It is seen in the *Chamaleon* tables and stools, designed by Terry Pecora for the Italian manufacturer Edra, where fabric is used to create the volume. The forms are dressed up. So much has become soft in the New Baroque, upholstered and padded. Robert Wettstein pads his hat racks, and in the process finds a new form. Upholstery becomes an art form with designs such as the *Tatlin* sofa by Mario Cananzi and Roberto Semprini for Edra. The *Tatlin,* inspired by the Russian constructivist from whom it takes its name, is also reminiscent of the opulent round sofas that filled palatial hotel lobbies at the turn of the last century, partly because of its lush red covering which seems more *luxe* than Marx. The New Baroque replaces leather and exposed steel frames with satin and velvet; color changes from gray and beige to a deep range of blues, purples, and greens. Robert le Héros and Garouste and Bonetti for Etamine use large, painterly prints with allegorical inspirations to swathe windows in fantasy and mystery.

In the amusing and ethereal fabric designs of Robert le Héros, angels and mythic heroes float through clouds, and across raging seas, each voyage captured with all of its passion and adventure in the narrative textiles designed by the group comprised of four women: Christelle Le Dean, Blandine Lelong, Isabelle Rodier, and Corinne Hellein. Each is a textile designer, born in 1962; they joined together in 1986 to create Robert le Héros (their logo is a crown above the initials RLH). Their designs, with titles such as *Sous le signe de Neptune* (Under the Sign of Neptune) and *Ton bonhomme qui tombe* (Your Gentleman Who Falls), deal with themes of astrology, discovery, and the sea. Some designs recount

Above: *Soleil* (sun) door handles, Robert le Héros, 1991, produced for Elisée Editions. Photograph courtesy of Elisée Editions.

Below: Shop window and fabrics, Nobilis, Paris, designed by Robert le Héros, 1991. Photograph by Bruno Clergue.

HOULE

entire folk tales; others resemble Renaissance interpretations of Greek myth. Robert le Héros use fabrics of large repeats and carpets to build new epics of their own creation. Often they work as stylists, draping a space, a store window, or an exhibition with their characters, painted heroes, and objects. They put a great deal of emphasis on the collection, that is, the assemblage of designs, patterns, and colors used together to create the fantasy.

Opposite, Above, Right, and Below: Fabric designs, Robert le Héros, 1989, manufactured by Nobilis. Photographs courtesy of Nobilis.

Above: *Astrid* and *Lola* metal garden chairs, Sylvia Corrette, 1991, manufactured by Fermob. Photograph courtesy of Fermob.

Below and Right: *Theodora* carpets (details), Sylvia Corrette, 1990, produced by Editions Philippe Laïk. Photographs courtesy of Philippe Laïk.

Above: *Roxanne Princesse des Djinns* stool, Sylvia Corrette, 1989, produced in a limited edition by VIA/Fermob. Photograph courtesy of VIA.

Right: *Roxanne Princesse des Djinns* chair, Sylvia Corrette, 1989, produced in a limited edition by VIA/Fermob. Photograph courtesy of VIA.

Below: *Roxanne Princesse des Djinns* table, Sylvia Corrette, 1989, produced in a limited edition by VIA/Fermob. Photograph courtesy of VIA.

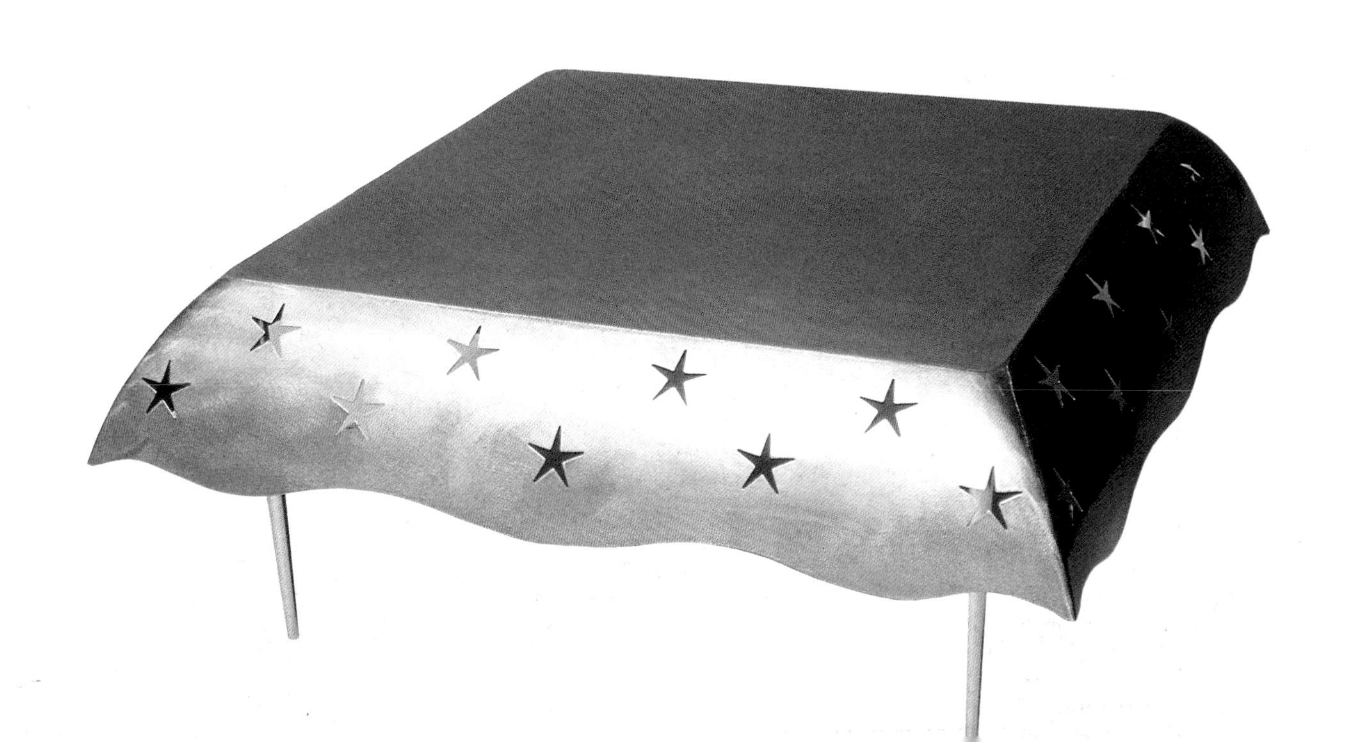

Fantastic and fable-inspired themes also pervade the work of designer Sylvia Corrette. Her *Roxanne Princesse des Djinns* is a thronelike chair for a mythical princess. This chair and matching stool were prototypes originally financed by VIA; the chair sold within a year, as a collector's item, at Paris's Drouot auction house. Corrette's next creations still had the dreams of palaces and starry nights. A painted wood cabinet for VIA and metal garden chairs for Fermob won her the title of Young Creator of the Year at the 1991 Paris Furniture Fair. Corrette's work frees our desire to dream, to fill our homes with little bits of fantasy. As Descartes said, "The charm of Fables awakens the mind."[8]

More often than not, however, fables include a dark side. While Corrette's designs seem far from dark, she is addressing an incertitude which she feels marks the end of this century. "It is a sentiment," she remarks, "that parallels the feelings of man one thousand years ago." Medieval man had a distrust of new discoveries and prophesied the end of the world as he understood it. Today, again there is a mistrust of the new, the high-tech, and a search for a deeper meaning. Far from being afraid to confront topics which seem touchy, emotional, and not, until recently, in the vocabulary of serious designers, Corrette greets the change as a spiritual muse. For Corrette, who studied history at the Sorbonne before getting a degree in interior design, there are always correlations to be made among history, literature, and the present which, as they affect our lives, affect her designs.

Before Corrette designs, she draws. In her drawings one can trace the confrontations between demons and fairies which inspire her work. Her richly colored drawings seem like either illustrations from a children's book or from medieval illuminated manuscripts. In fact, it is from the illuminated works that she finds much of her inspiration. She wraps her drawings with quotes from medieval writings or, quite often, from Charles Baudelaire, the modern poet in the streets of Paris, seeking the spiritual which included the dark and the light. Corrette sees in Baudelaire a violence; although she herself has never felt adept at putting words to paper, she has found through Baudelaire a way to express the violent in her own subconscious. "In each poem" she says, "there is a scream coming from Baudelaire." To take his words is to find "a way to let out my scream." Baudelaire is not so much an inspiration as a text to which she often refers, a text already embedded in her being. Yet, it is evident in her work that she is far from obsessed with the pain in life; inspirations also come from other parts of the world, as can be seen in her Byzantine carpet design for Philippe Laïk.

Above: *Les Enluminés* cabinet, Sylvia Corrette, 1991, prototype produced for VIA. Photograph courtesy of VIA.

Opposite: *Calypso* metal garden chair, Sylvia Corrette, 1991, manufactured by Fermob. Photograph courtesy of Fermob.

New Baroque design is found in the textile design of carpets and fabrics, and in decorative objects from door knobs to mirrors. Small bronze objects by Franck Evennou, or Gerard Dalmon's door handles, have little to do with industrial design and everything to do with the *beau objet*. Nothing has been invented, only made attractive. The object is "designed," that is, made by someone who is an artist and not a machine. This gives a whole new meaning to the word "designed." Where one once said "crafted," or simply "made by," one now says "designed by." Design with a capital *D* is the follower to Art with a capital *A*.

Design, particularly the New Baroque, is very fashionable. It is fashionable to be knowledgeable of design and designers, and it is fashionable to design. The New Baroque sets a stage for the superabundance of contemporary images; at the edge of the stage is the director, the designer/promoter, the promoter of style, of a "look," or of what is called the total design concept. Alexis Lahellec of Paris designs furniture as part of a total involvement with creation, an involvement which includes his collection of jewelry and decorative objects for the home. Lahellec has put the growing interest in

Above: Mirror, Franck Evennou, 1991, produced in a limited edition for Galerie de l'Objet Insolite. Photograph courtesy of Galerie de l'Objet Insolite.

Right: Door knobs and handles produced for Galerie de l'Objet Insolite for "Nouvelles Poignées de Porte" exhibition, October—November 1990, designed by (clockwise from top left) Augustin Granet, Gérard Dalmon, Frédérique Morrel, J.B. Sibertin Blanc, Kalinger, Delphine Kohler, Migeon and Migeon, Christine Lievin, and Kalinger. Photograph courtesy of Galerie de l'Objet Insolite.

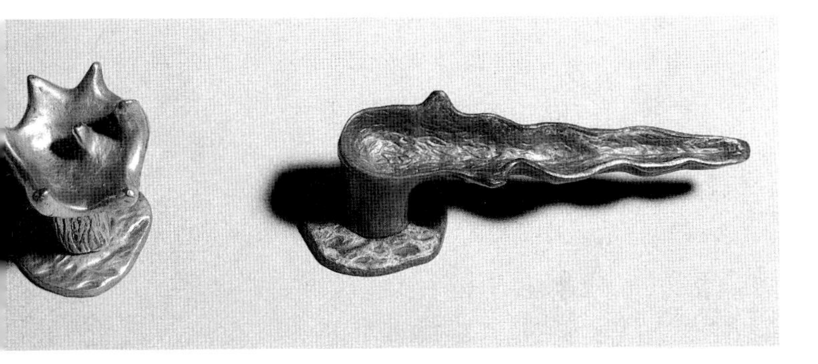

Above: Door knob and handle, Gérard Dalmon, 1989, produced for Neotu. Photograph courtesy of Neotu.

Right: Wall torch, Franck Evennou, 1991, produced in a limited edition for Elisée Editions. Photograph courtesy of Elisée Editions.

Below: *Lune* (moon) bench, Franck Evennou, 1991, produced in a limited edition for Elisée Editions. Photograph courtesy of Elisée Editions.

Above: *Etoile* (star) stool, Franck Evennou, 1991, produced in a limited edition for Elisée Editions. Photograph courtesy of Elisée Editions.

Above: Picture frame, Franck Evennou, 1989, produced for En Attendant les Barbares. Photograph by Denis Menou.

Below: *L'Ile au Tresor* (Treasure Island) carpet (detail), Franck Evennou, 1991, produced in a limited edition for Elisée Editions. Photograph courtesy of Elisée Editions.

Left: *Bikila* cuckoo clock, Alexis Lahellec, 1989, produced in a limited edition for Alexis Lahellec boutiques. Photograph courtesy of Alexis Lahellec.

Below: *Issangar* sofa, Alexis Lahellec, 1990, produced in a limited series for Alexis Lahellec boutiques. Photograph courtesy of Alexis Lahellec.

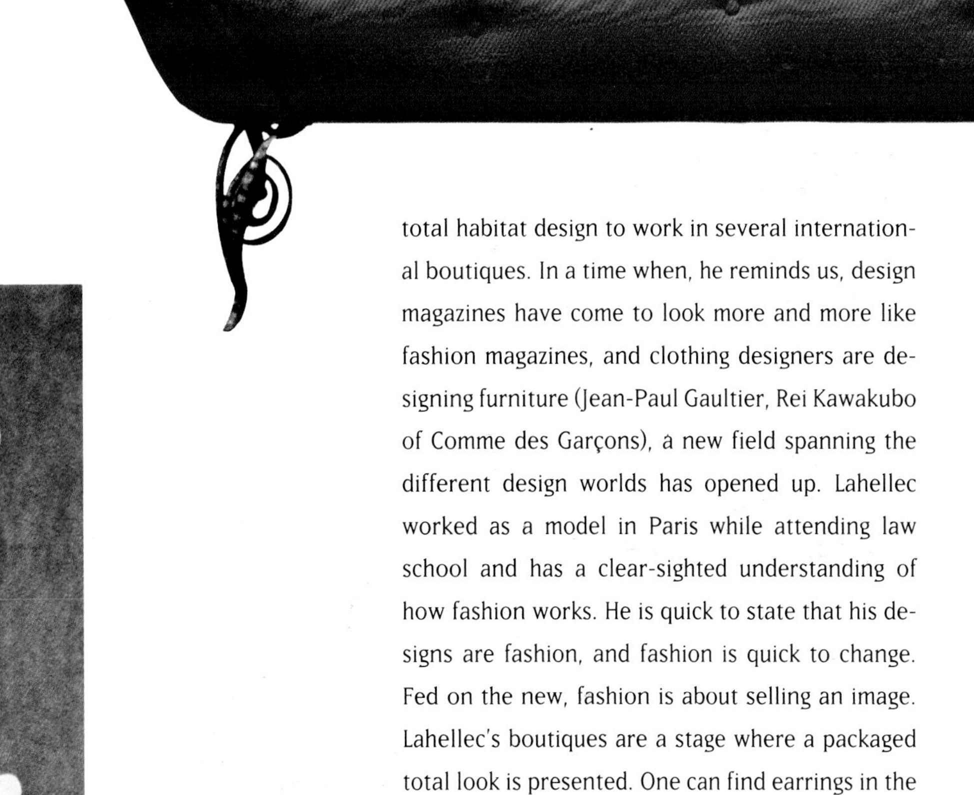

total habitat design to work in several international boutiques. In a time when, he reminds us, design magazines have come to look more and more like fashion magazines, and clothing designers are designing furniture (Jean-Paul Gaultier, Rei Kawakubo of Comme des Garçons), a new field spanning the different design worlds has opened up. Lahellec worked as a model in Paris while attending law school and has a clear-sighted understanding of how fashion works. He is quick to state that his designs are fashion, and fashion is quick to change. Fed on the new, fashion is about selling an image. Lahellec's boutiques are a stage where a packaged total look is presented. One can find earrings in the

same collection, with the same theme, as a stool. Lahellec is trying to assert neither permanence nor importance. He is a designer and a promoter. He is also a very savvy and attractive man who is as much a part of the ideal package as his designs. The New Baroque puts a tremendous emphasis on the designer, who is himself fashionable, sellable. This is the connection of fashion and the New Baroque. As Lahellec says, "I accept the superficial [and] do what amuses."

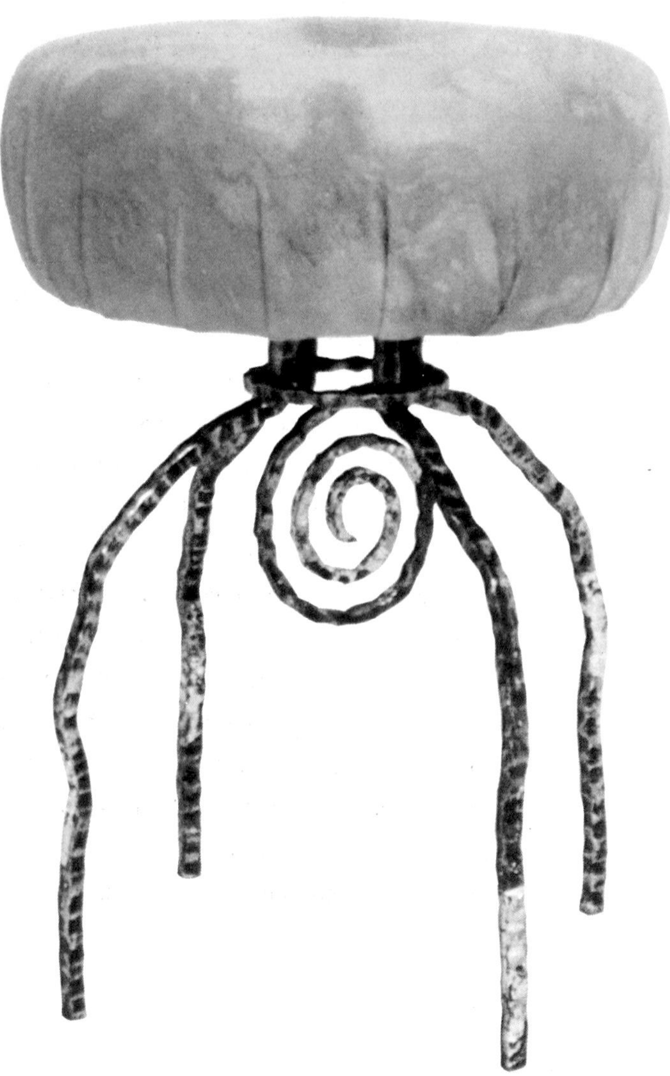

Above: *Nyamau* sofa, Alexis Lahellec, 1989, produced in a limited edition for Alexis Lahellec boutiques. Photograph courtesy of Alexis Lahellec.

Right: *Dia-Ba* stool, Alexis Lahellec, 1989, produced in a limited edition for Alexis Lahellec boutiques. Photograph courtesy of Alexis Lahellec.

A rethinking of the superficial is at the root of the New Baroque. Is the superficial all bad? Not if it is put to the test of our cultural realities. In other words, the superficial is a part of life that can be used positively. Further, not all that glitters is superficial, hype, or fake. This prejudice was instilled in designers by the early modernist treatises. Purity, which came to mean puritanical, was a symbol of elitist design. While the rest of the art community has long left this standard behind, furniture design has taken a little more time to find a way to be functional and saturated with symbols of modern excess at the same time. A prime example would be the ornate lamps and chandeliers of Toni Cordero for Artemide. Cordero merges technology with the baroque as he hangs spirals of chromed metal with multicolored glass and crystal drops. For Artemide, a lighting company that represents some of the modern masterpieces of our time, the plunge into the New Baroque is further proof that modern design is always emerging, always being redefined.

The New Baroque must be differentiated from the concept of postmodernism from the start, that is, the general architectural definition of postmodernism which has carried over to all facets of design. This definition implies that the "post" is a reaction to the modernist style, which, within its frame of rationalism, disallowed any movement but a single line towards abstraction. Postmodern design looked to history and resurrected the facade, the entry, and decoration. It easily turned into a pastiche of parts. The architectural definition of postmodernism, extolled by writers such as Charles Jencks, is confused with the cultural definition of postmodern, which reflects an overall societal reliance on the simulacrum, the mask, for its primary source of knowledge. Each definition, however, accepts a certain cover-up of reality. The New Baroque, along with the other tendencies discussed in this book, is separated from the postmodern debate by the same turn from formalism that separated it from the modern style. Whether it be the pure object or the decorated shed (to quote Robert Venturi), neither the form nor the mask is the concern. The concern is the desire to act, to physically involve, and to communicate in the lexicon of the storyteller.

Above: *Astrea* chandelier, Toni Cordero, 1990, manufactured by Artemide. Photograph courtesy of Artemide.

Right: *Cipria* chandelier, Toni Cordero, 1990, manufactured by Artemide. Photograph courtesy of Artemide.

Below: *Latona* floor lamp, Toni Cordero, 1990, manufactured by Artemide. Photograph courtesy of Artemide.

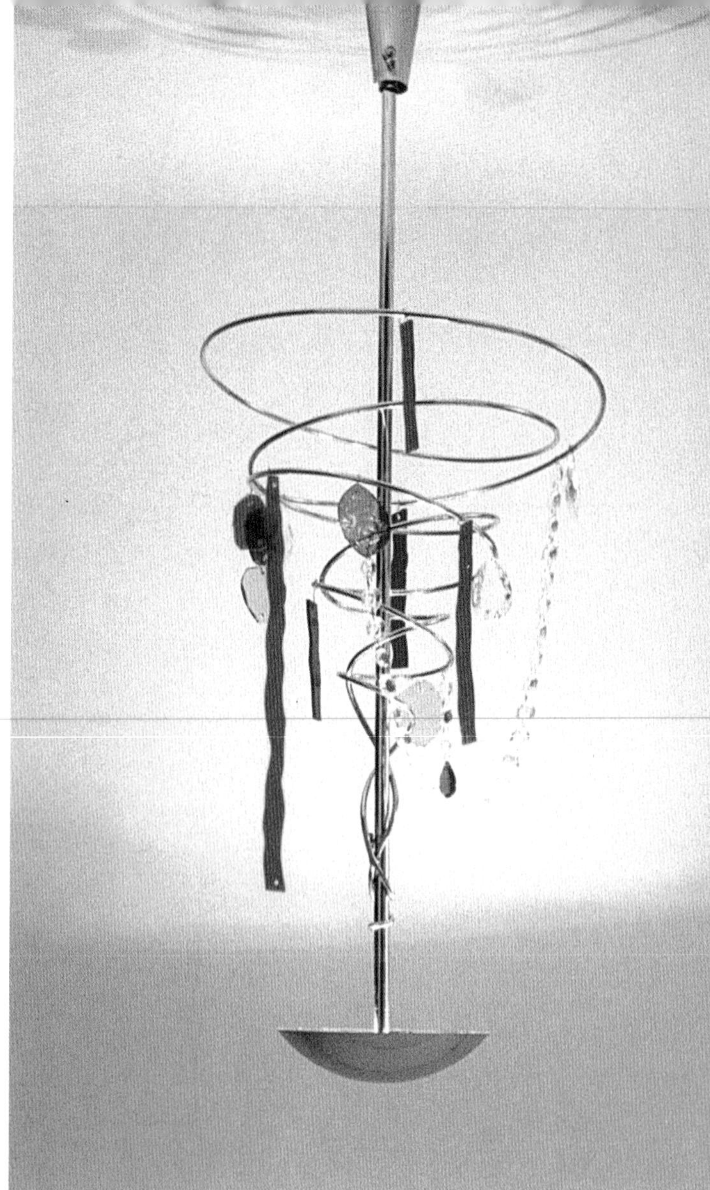

Perhaps we have merely gone back to early modern times, in the spirit of modern thinkers such as Piranesi or Manet, who used a collage of recognizable "quotations" to announce their move into new territory. In other words, they referenced their own point of departure. What we have experienced from Manet to the present is a period of design history that lost the ability to impose its own cultural identity upon itself. Manet was quick to capture the manner and events of his time in his work as he contributed a new manner of seeing to the world of art. A furniture designer, through more gestural and tactile ways, can attempt the same dialogue. Unlike postmodern architects, whose work consciously cited preexisting examples such as Doric or Tuscan architecture, designers such as Garouste and Bonetti are rarely so studious or direct in their inspirations. Theirs is an invention for invention's sake—the route of the artist.

Below left and Below: Chairs from the *Reggenza* collection, Toni Cordero, 1991, manufactured by Morphos. Photographs courtesy of Morphos.

The name New Baroque creates its own hazards. But words in themselves are based on historical reference. After all, the word *baroque* does conjure up all sorts of favorable impressions that we have not indulged in for some time. Baroque does, however, retain a formal connotation of Italian churches and French gardens—a courtliness which designers have revived. Baroque is most often, in this book, meant as a dynamic, the spirit of universal explorations and movement. Only the limitation of words can distract us from the aim.

Above: *Ifigenia* table lamp, Toni Cordero, 1990, manufactured by Artemide. Photograph courtesy of Artemide.

Right: Stool from the *Reggenza* collection, Toni Cordero, 1991, manufactured by Morphos. Photograph courtesy of Morphos.

Opposite: Chair from the *Reggenza* collection, Toni Cordero, 1991, manufactured by Morphos. Photograph courtesy of Morphos.

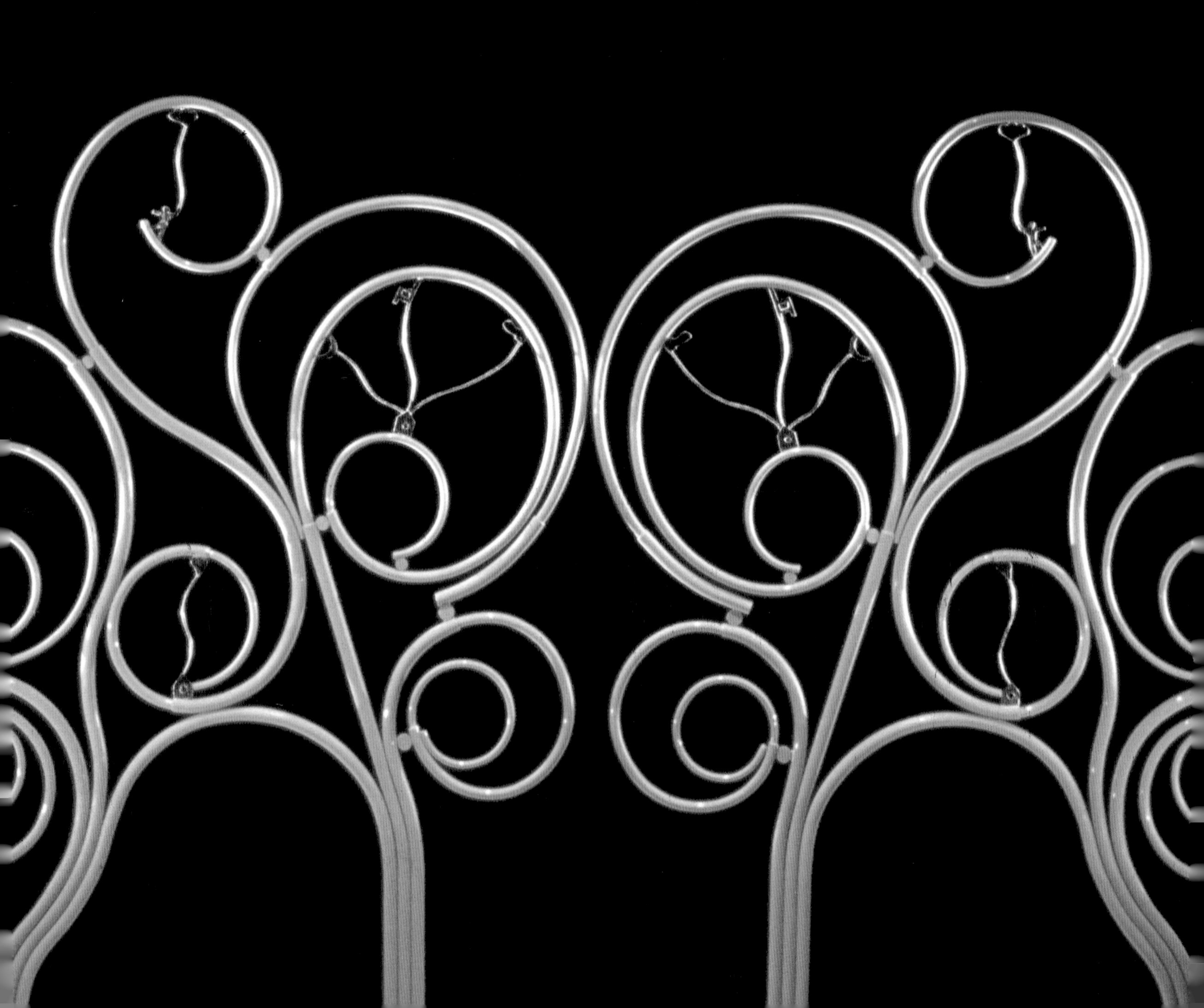

The New Naturalism

Nature is contributing a romanticism, perhaps even a sense of folly, to design. The connection in modern design to urban images, to the fast, the hard, the aggressive, has become a trap. Is the presence of nature, of poetry, somehow less important, less credible? Not if one thinks of the inherent tension in nature between violence and beauty. The New Naturalism is not a naive vision but a strong critical statement, often with more than a bit of humor, that places nature in a state of suspended animation within our man-made interiors.

There is no compulsion in designers of a postwar, post-industrial, postmodern Europe to work in natural materials in order to simulate nature. Instead, the materials are often the signs of a society that destroys and wastes. Andrea Branzi's neon light for Memphis is a luminous leaf that can be applied to a wall, a ceiling, anywhere a ghostly memory of nature can bring the interior into surreal contact with the exterior. The message is a technical replacement of the original, a neon signboard that says "nature exists," it is out there. The strength of Branzi's design is that nature does continue to survive and it is instantly recognizable in the most abstract or reconstructed images.

Andrea Branzi is an Italian architect and critic and one of the founders of Domus Academy, the Milan design school. His *Domestic Animals* collection, produced in 1985–86, took a divergent stance from the world of rational or supposedly post-industrial design. A collection of furniture half made by machine, half of tree branches, comes as if from nowhere. Branzi says of his collection, "They make use of primitive archetypal symbols and materials, in conformity with a canon of myth, to produce emotional effects." In each piece in the collection the strength lies in the striking contrast between brute gestures and emotions.

"The title 'Domestic Animals,'" says Branzi, "should be understood as a sort of metaphor of the relationship that links man to a number of animal (but also technical) presences within his home. Just as animals can be a positive presence in our habitat, so too technological inventions can be 'domesticated,' that is, rendered suitable for sharing man's most private spaces."[9] Along with this domestication comes a new understanding of the dwelling as a unique living space whose rituals mirror neither those of the workplace nor those of the street. His collection reflects both a research into the New Naturalism and a Primitive domesticity. Branzi, in fact, labeled the *Domestic Animals* collection "neo-primitive," a style which brings together the technological objects of everyday life—the television, the toaster—with the rediscovery of naturalism.

The designs of *Domestic Animals* include several chairs and benches with birch-branch backs, a table with metal "bamboo" supports painted purple, and a bookcase/shed with antlers over the door. Later, turning towards the cultivated garden, Branzi designed the *Iudolia* bench, in which he combined the mundane garden bench and fence in a reinvestigation of pastoral simplicity, complete with the same rabbit character, painted on the bench back, that was the logo for *Domestic Animals.* The rabbit is the tamed wild animal to whom Branzi has given a very human face.

Designs like the *Iudolia* bench carry with them an inherent critique of modern design and production. They offer a heroic normality as an antithesis to all that is overly processed and lacking humanity. The idea is not to live without technology, but to live better with it. Too often, however, living in increasingly hectic, business-oriented cities like Branzi's own Milan leaves the urbanite with a void, or monotony, in his environment. He needs other images on which to dream, images as those on Branzi's *Neolia* headboard, a transparent screen with floating birds and plants. These images from nature bring to mind the art of Matisse, who rendered nature in a similar primitive, animated style. In each case the expression of emotion takes over. Branzi delves into the gap between meaning and object. He is designing for the urban gardener, he who cultivates the poetry amid the machinery and noise of daily existence.

Opposite: *Metopa* headboard (detail), Riccardo Dalisi, 1989, manufactured in a limited edition by Zanotta. Photograph courtesy of Zanotta.

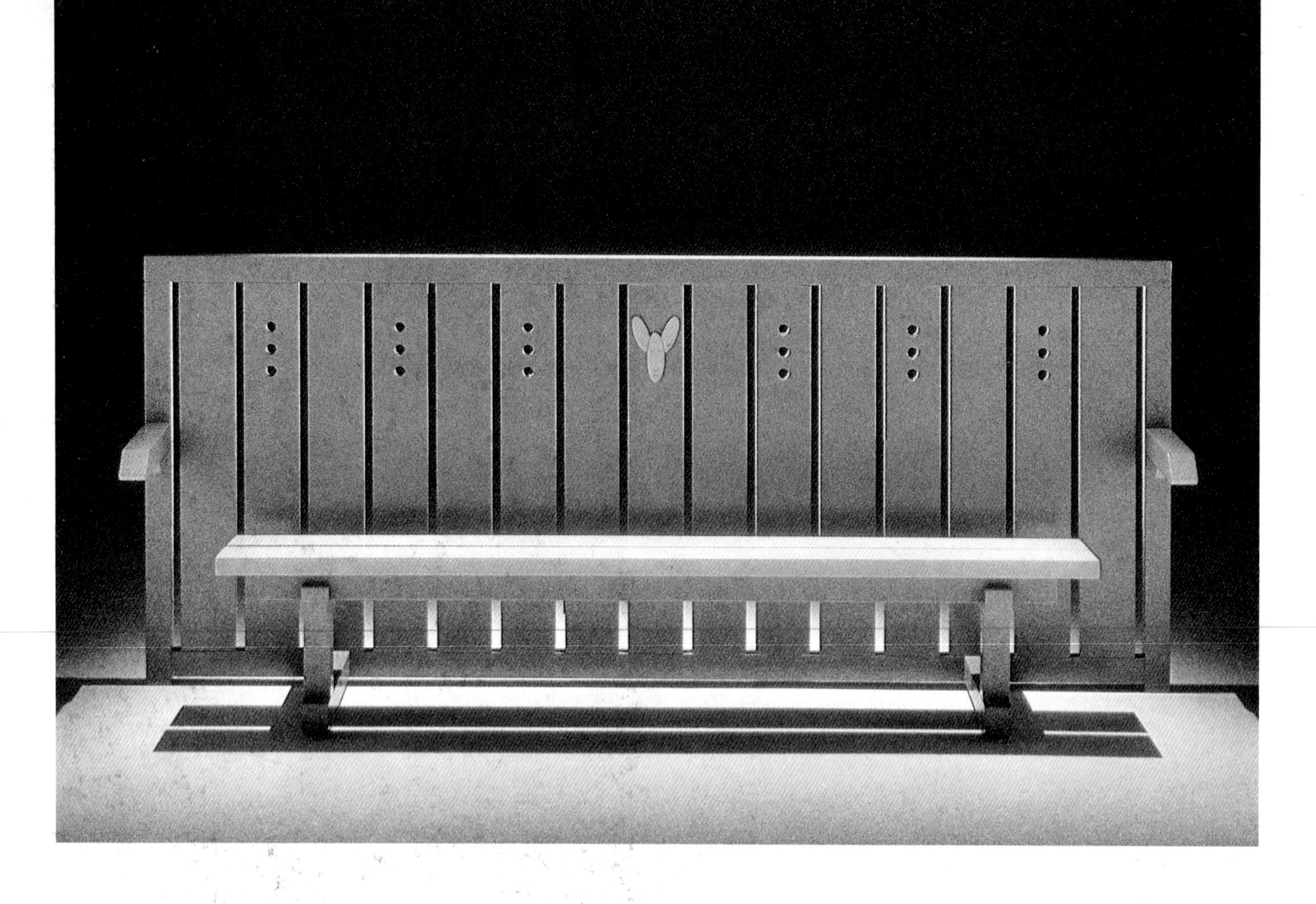

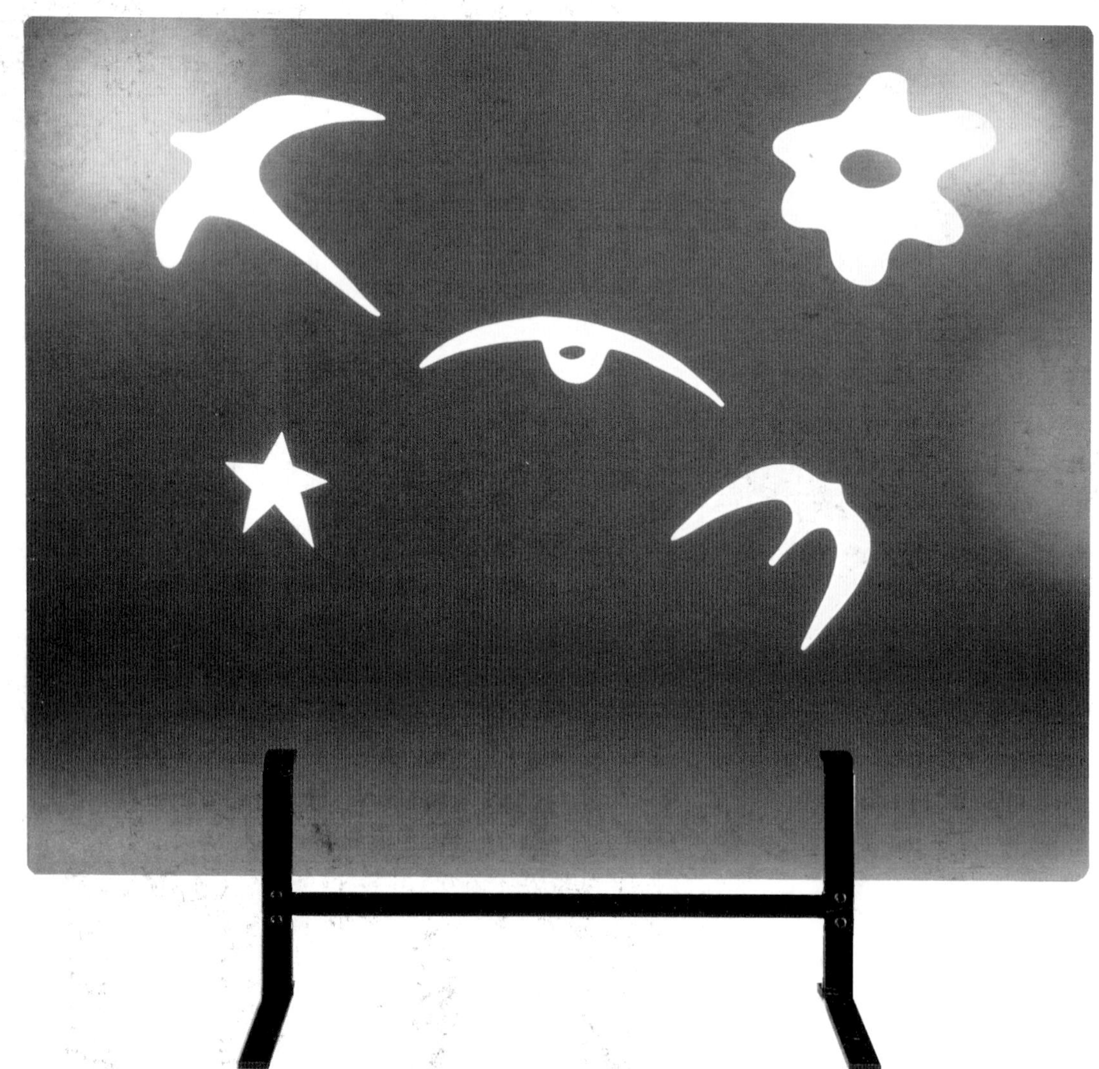

Opposite, top: *Iudolia* bench, Andrea Branzi, 1989, manufactured in a limited edition by Zanotta. Photograph courtesy of Zanotta.

Opposite, bottom: *Neolia* headboard, Andrea Branzi, 1989, manufactured in a limited edition by Zanotta. Photograph courtesy of Zanotta.

Right and Below: Chairs from the *Domestic Animals* collection, Andrea Branzi, 1985, manufactured by Zabro. Photographs by Emilio Tremolada.

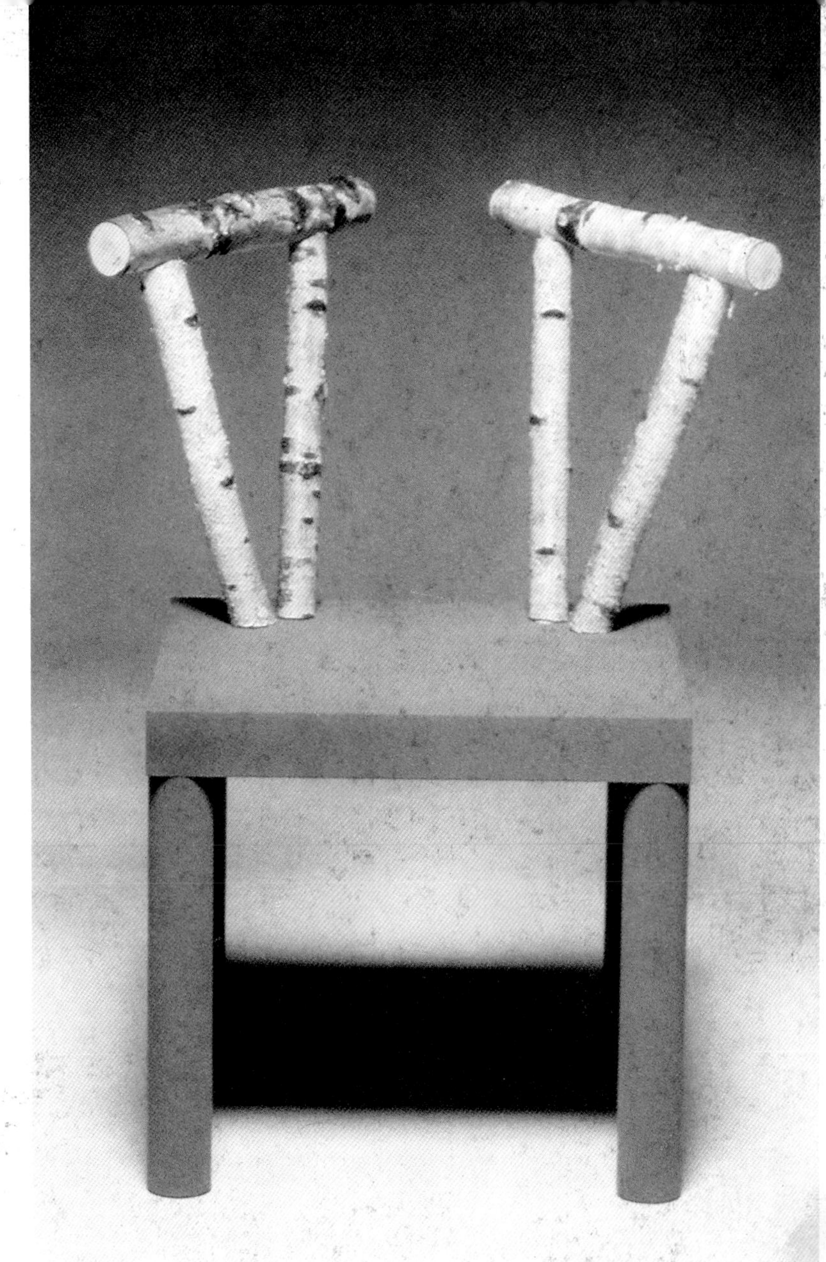

Above: *Domestic Animals* collection exhibition, Museo Alchimia, Milan, 1985, interior and furniture designed by Andrea Branzi. Photograph by Emilio Tremolada.

Below: *Foglia* neon light fixture, Andrea Branzi, 1988, produced by Memphis Milano. Photograph by Santi Caleca.

Left: *Alsaziano* bookcase from the *Domestic Animals* collection, Andrea Branzi, 1985, manufactured by Zabro. Photograph by Emilio Tremolada.

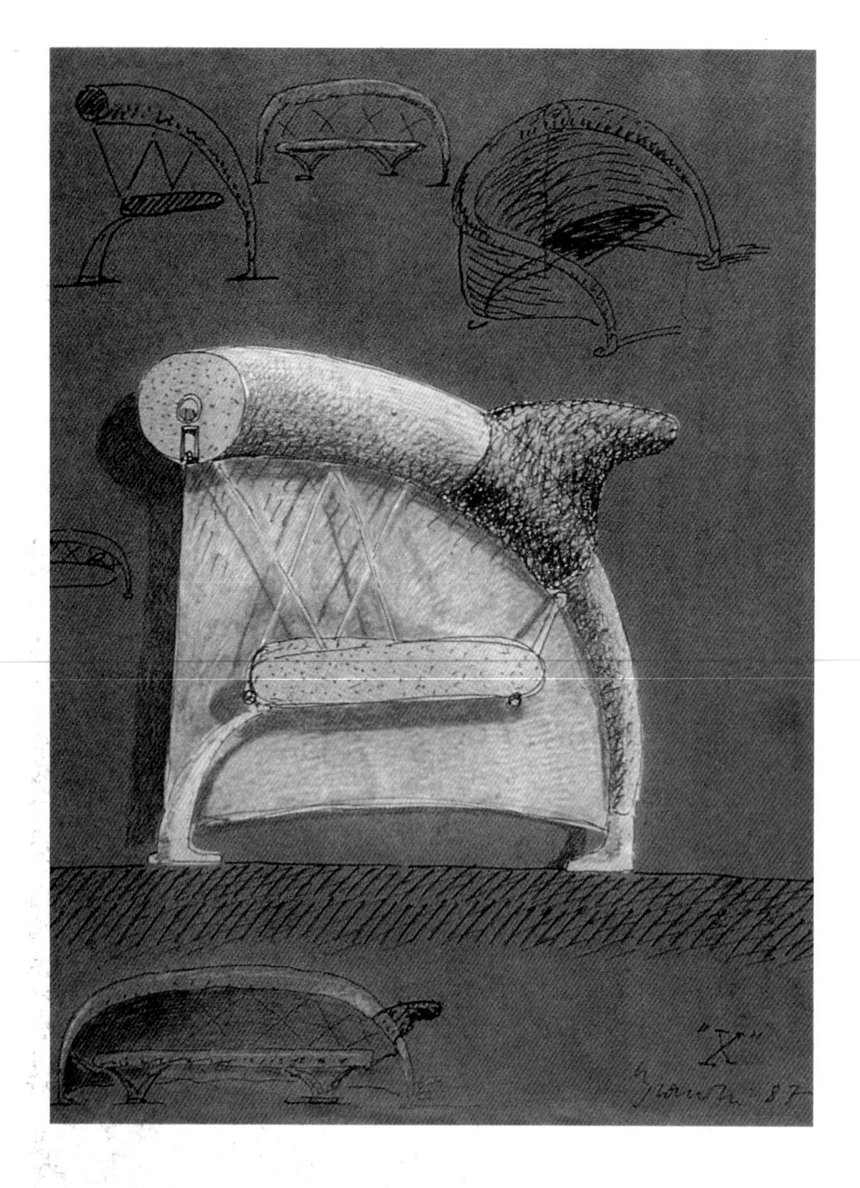

Left: Drawing of *Axale* sofa for Cassina, Andrea Branzi, 1989. Photograph courtesy of Andrea Branzi.

Below: Drawing of *Berione* bookshelves for Cassina, Andrea Branzi, 1989. Photograph courtesy of Andrea Branzi.

Left: Flower stand from the *Domestic Animals* collection, Andrea Branzi, 1985, manufactured by Zabro. Photograph by Emilio Tremolada.

Below: *Pavone* chair, Riccardo Dalisi, 1986, manufactured in a limited edition by Zanotta. Photograph courtesy of Zanotta.

Andrea Branzi and Riccardo Dalisi are just two of the designers creating a limited series of pieces for the Italian manufacturer Zanotta. Dalisi's whimsical creations—a bird chair, a butterfly bench—create a zoological fantasy for the interior or the garden. In brightly painted metal he fashions his creatures: *Pavone,* a two-headed peacock catching the proverbial worm in its two yellow beaks; *Mariposa,* looking ready to fold its blue steel wings at any moment; *Metopa,* green metal vines curling in romantic tendrils on a headboard. They are sculpture (more inviting when seen rather than used), studies in the unique object, or what happens when a chair becomes a bird, and so on. The difference is sometimes subtle between designs that begin as a formal study and those that begin as a means of correspondence between object, man, space, habitat, and ritual. At the beginning of a new design movement, we are often caught in a conflict between our love of certain "well-designed" and beautiful objects, and a desire for something more, something to bridge the gap between real life and expectation.

Above: *Fiordalisi* chairs, Riccardo Dalisi, 1991, manufactured by Morphos. Photograph courtesy of Morphos.

Right: *Fiordalisi* chair (detail), Riccardo Dalisi, 1991, manufactured by Morphos. Photograph courtesy of Morphos.

Opposite: *Mariposa* bench, Riccardo Dalisi, 1989, manufactured in a limited edition by Zanotta. Photograph courtesy of Zanotta.

Above: *Metopa* headboard, Riccardo Dalisi, 1989, manufactured in a limited edition by Zanotta. Photograph courtesy of Zanotta.

Italian design, since its domination of the design industry throughout the 1970s and 1980s, is often straddling the gap between the burden and the gift of its design legacy. One of the Italian design "masters" is Alessandro Mendini, who has joined in the experiment in New Naturalism and created (for Zanotta) the daisy-topped *Hispo* table, which melts into an amorphic green base. Mendini, along with Dalisi, was among the original members of Studio Alchimia in the late 1970s. Later, joined by Andrea Branzi, Ettore Sottsass, and others, Alchimia designed furniture with a critical edge which changed the face of Italian design. They resurrected the banal object, fascinated by the challenge of bridging the gap between popular and modern design. They also investigated the idea of decoration as design, not simply as application or as an afterthought to a completed idea. Yet, underlying rational forms (right angles) and the concerns of standardization and production still characterized their work. Zanotta, which continues to create furniture by these designers, has followed their evolution from neo-modernist concerns to a new concern for the artist's place in the creation of unique designs. Speaking of a now neo-industrial world, Zanotta biographer Stefano Casciani writes that design "can no longer be thought of only in terms of unlimited repetitions of the same shape but also of unlimited possibilities of formal and material variations." The result is work that arrives at an ability to express "metaphors of the present,"[10] metaphors which have become more naturalistic, more human.

Throughout this book we see the forms of nature, specifically animal nature (the Primitive gazelles of Cherif, and the humorous seated cow of Nigel Coates, for example). Each in its own way is looking to build a rapport with the user. In his collection *Gallo Galleggio Gallino Gallone,* Nigel Coates has designed furniture that "works at elaborating experience, not just decorating or functionalizing it." His *Galleggio* sofa and the rest of the collection incorporate pieces from wings, claws, and animal haunches to put the user in contact with something he instinctively feels comfortable with. "Almost any piece of furniture," says Coates, "from the school bench to the love seat, embodies the anthropomorphic spirit. My furniture always plays up this aspect. I think that any piece of furniture should solicit affection, not just as a picture in a magazine, but as a territory of experience. Though neither pets nor lovers, chairs can be part of our psychological scenario." These designs, of course, are based on a man-and-animal relationship, one that has long existed, but has rarely been turned into such usable furniture.

Even in cultivated plant life, the imagery of nature is powerful. The soft, giant flower chairs of Masanori Umeda for Edra are seductive. His *Rose Chair*, for example, is in full bloom, with just enough space within its layers of plump, plush petals to support one person in what is a surreal or even Lilliputian experience—an interaction with an object that is at once unnatural (one does not sit on flowers) and magical. Umeda's flowers speak on the level of animation, rather than sculpture. By embracing the form, color, and spirit of nature, Umeda's designs have added a new dimension to the narrative of New Design, one which infuses interior space with memory and poetry, one which understands the interior impressionistically rather than structurally, as a stage for the event of living. These designs also demonstrate a willingness among Italian manufacturers to take risks to render complex designs, and to build them with enviable craftsmanship. Umeda has been working in Italy, notably with Memphis, since 1982. At that time, he produced *Ginza*, a type of cabinet modeled on a robot; now he has turned from the mechanized idealization of the human form to the sources of nature itself. The invitation to sit on the flowers is evident in the form; if one is still hesitant to do so, it is because of the old injunction not to touch.

Below: *Galleggio* sofa, Nigel Coates, 1991, manufactured by Poltronova. Photograph courtesy of Poltronova.

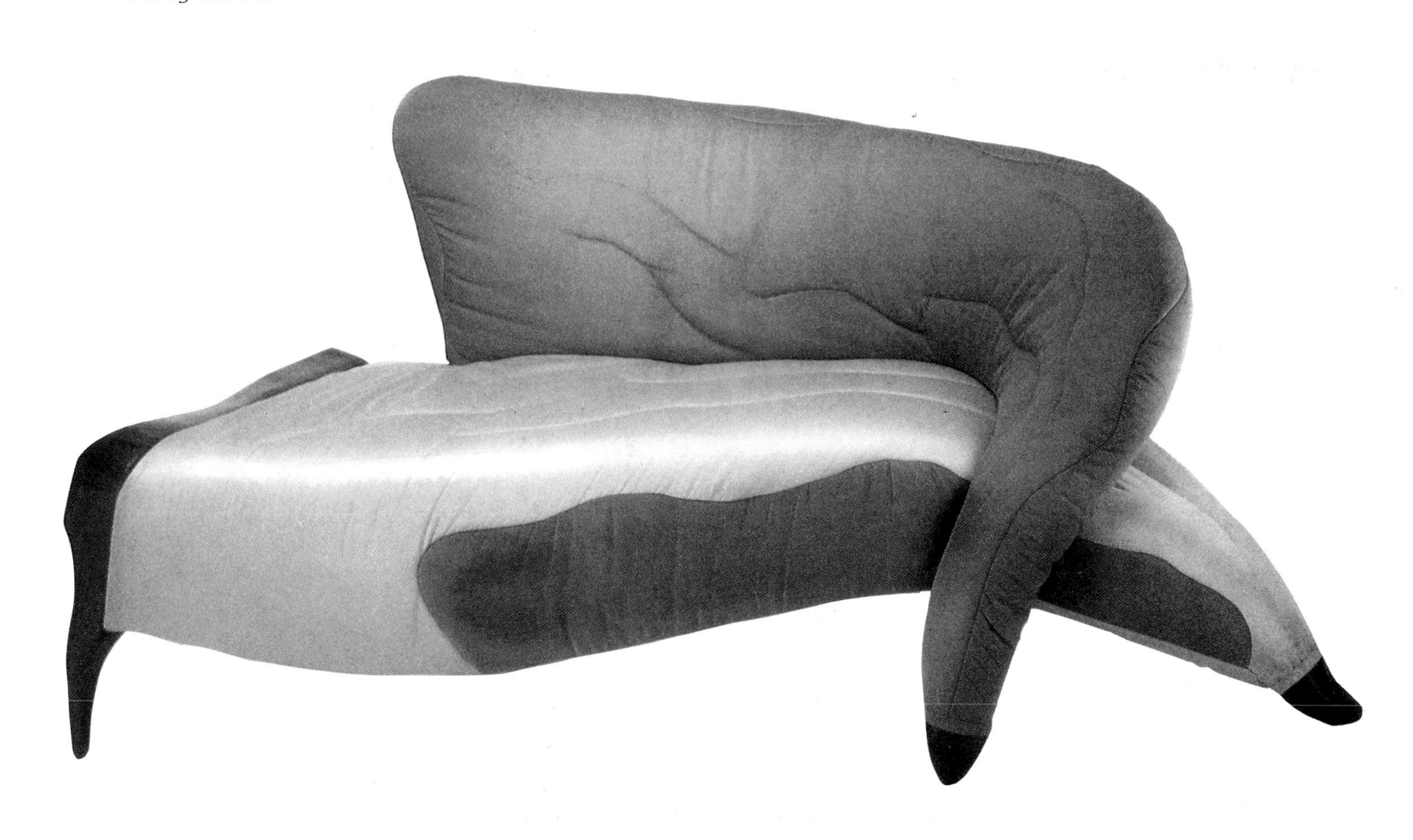

Left: *Gallo* armchair, Nigel Coates, 1991, manufactured by Poltronova. Photograph courtesy of Poltronova.

Below: Collection of flower-shaped chairs (including prototypes), Masanori Umeda, 1990, manufactured by Edra. Photograph courtesy of Edra.

Right: *Getsuen* chair, Masanori Umeda, 1990, manufactured by Edra. Photograph courtesy of Edra.

Below: *Rose Chair*, Masanori Umeda, 1990, manufactured by Edra. Photograph courtesy of Edra.

Moving from the softness of stuffed flowers to the jagged lines of sea coral, Garouste and Bonetti's *Trapani* collection exaggerates nature's structure, form, and color, blowing them up to an unnatural scale. These designs, as Umeda's flowers, are toylike, an effect which stems from the exploded scale, vibrant color, and the intense unreality of each piece. Here a blue deeper than the Mediterranean and an orange more aggressive than its coral reefs come alive in the same sense that trees talk and flowers sing in films, cartoons, and the latest fad gadgets. These lamps, sofas, and chairs do not actually move, and they are certainly more elegant than singing flowers, but they are full of animation. The chair and sofa seats are extra thick, and heavy bolsters form the back and arms. The big geometric shapes are then joined by the coral branches. One long branch stands upright to create the floor lamp; then the whole game is changed, as the coral is reduced in scale for the tableware collection for Daum. The name *Trapani* comes from a Sicilian village where small objects have been made from coral for centuries. Garouste and Bonetti have found in Trapani an inspiration, from which, as is their usual habit, they have begun their own tradition.

Right: Floor lamp from the *Trapani* collection, Garouste and Bonetti, 1989, produced in a limited edition by VIA and Galerie Lieux. Photograph courtesy of VIA.

Above and Right: Chair and ottoman from the *Trapani* collection, Garouste and Bonetti, 1989, produced in a limited edition by VIA and Galerie Lieux. Photographs courtesy of VIA.

Above: Tableware and candelabra in *pâte de verre* from the *Trapani* collection, Garouste and Bonetti, 1990, manufactured by Daum. Photograph courtesy of Daum.

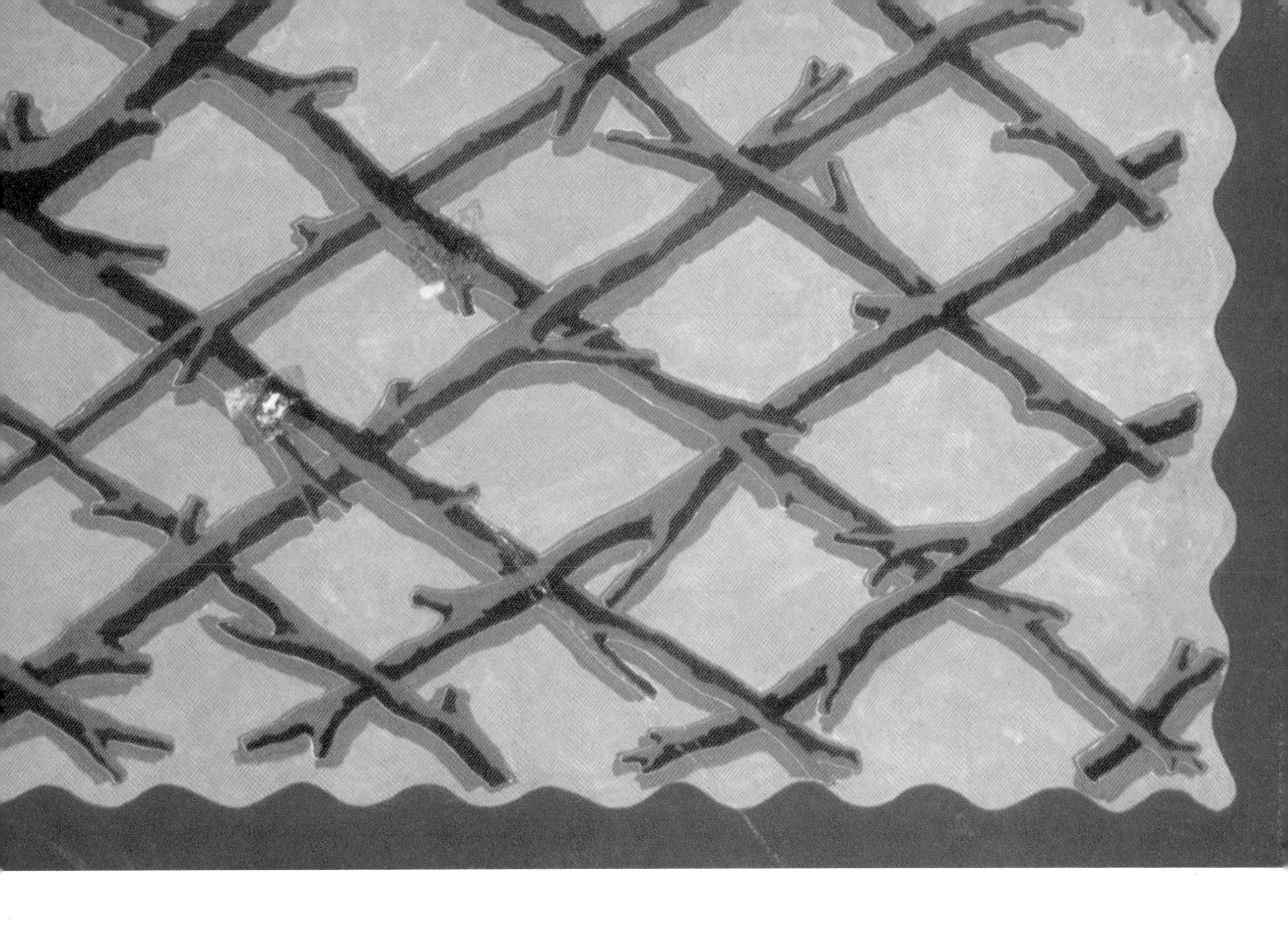

Above: Carpet from the *Trapani* collection (detail), Garouste and Bonetti, 1989, produced in a limited edition by VIA and Galerie Lieux. Photograph courtesy of VIA.

Left: Sofa from the *Trapani* collection, Garouste and Bonetti, 1989, produced in a limited edition by VIA and Galerie Lieux. Photograph courtesy of VIA.

Nature can also be transformed into two-dimensional patterns. A variety of carpet designs from all corners of Europe use images of nature: Garouste and Bonetti have created daisy chains and fields of tulips for Philippe Laïk; Nanda Vigo has combined the abstract with the classic rose in his carpets for Driade Follies; Spanish artist and designer Javier Mariscal has put the tropics and beasts in his designs for Marieta. Each design demonstrates the ongoing renaissance in carpet design and manufacture. From limited-edition carpets by designers, produced at enormous cost, to those (sometimes by the same designer) that are more widely accessible, the market is expanding at all levels. The renewed interest in the rug as a decorative object comes after the decline in popularity of the wall-to-wall carpet, with its characteristically homogeneous treatment of surfaces, blending and smoothing the edges of a room by offering no resistance. As in most aspects of design today, the public has grown tired of sameness.

Designers have embraced carpet design as one more challenge within the continually merging fields of design. Such work does, however, require a certain study of the history of carpet design and an understanding of proportion, border, and field. The most successful designs have an affinity to these ideals within the realm of the two-dimensional, and take advantage of the new technology in tufting rugs, which has made possible the most complicated and free-flowing designs. Today, the artisan shoots the threads through the backing with a gun, without having to make a knot. The process of interpreting a design is faster and easier. The price is based not on the number of rugs made (they are each made by hand), but on the quality of materials and name value of the designer.

One of the most exclusive carpet collections is that of Yves Gastou. He invited designers from all over Europe, and the late Shiro Kuramata of Japan, to create "cartoons" or two-dimensional designs for carpets. Some of his most successful collaborations incorporate themes of nature and the earth, as in Sylvain Dubuisson's maze entitled *Initiation*. Dubuisson's classic garden maze—with a stylized rose at the center, a lifelike hand pointing to the challenge, and a sundial giving a fatalistic importance to the quest—demonstrates just how unlimited designs can be. It follows both the ancient tradition of carpets that tell a story or hold a message, and the structural direction of a centralized design. Andrea Branzi's design uses a field of irregular lines, those of a cracked and barren earth, punctuated by regular markers of some mystical orientation. *Tapis des Bois* (Carpet of the Woods) by Robert le Héros for Elisée Editions turns in another direction in an abstract rendering of woodland terrain with a demi-border of knotty branches. Even those of a more romantic design, such as Marco de Gueltzl's *Tapis de Feuilles* (Carpet of Leaves), where leaves float in a loose field across a luminous cream base, encircled by a border of gold threads, has a power that becomes the basis for a new attitude towards room design. What has arisen in New Design is an ability to weave the narrative with the product, to layer illusion on practicality, and to include nature in the urbane.

Above: *Belle Forêt* carpet, Garouste and Bonetti, 1990, produced for Editions Philippe Laïk. Photograph courtesy of Philippe Laïk.

Above: *Marguerites* carpet (detail), Garouste and Bonetti, 1990, produced for Editions Philippe Laïk. Photograph courtesy of Philippe Laïk.

Left: *Tulips* carpet, Garouste and Bonetti, 1990, produced for Editions Philippe Laïk. Photograph courtesy of Philippe Laïk.

Above, top: *Orian* carpet (detail), Nanda Vigo, late 1980s, manufactured by Driade Follies. Photograph by Leo Torri.

Above, center: *Theodore* carpet, Nanda Vigo, late 1980s, manufactured by Driade Follies. Photograph by Leo Torri.

Above, bottom: *Rohan* carpet, Nanda Vigo, late 1980s, manufactured by Driade Follies. Photograph by Leo Torri.

Opposite: *Tapis des Bois* (Carpet of the Woods, detail), Robert le Héros, 1990, produced in a limited edition for Elisée Editions. Photograph courtesy of Elisée Editions.

Above and Left: Carpets, Javier Mariscal, 1990, produced for Marieta. Photograph courtesy of Marieta.

Opposite: *Bouquets* carpet, Garouste and Bonetti, 1990, produced for Editions Philippe Laïk. Photograph courtesy of Philippe Laïk.

B.G

Opposite: *Tapis de Feuilles* (Carpet of Leaves), Marco de Gueltzl, 1990, produced in a limited edition for Elisée Editions. Photograph by Rauzier & Rivière.

Right: *Tapis du Ciel* (Carpet of the Sky), Robert le Héros, 1990, produced in a limited edition for Elisée Editions. Photograph courtesy of Elisée Editions.

Below: *Grains de Folie* (Seeds of Folly) carpet, Franck Evennou, 1991, produced by Wamba and distributed by Anne Shelton Gallery. Photograph by Heiner Troendle.

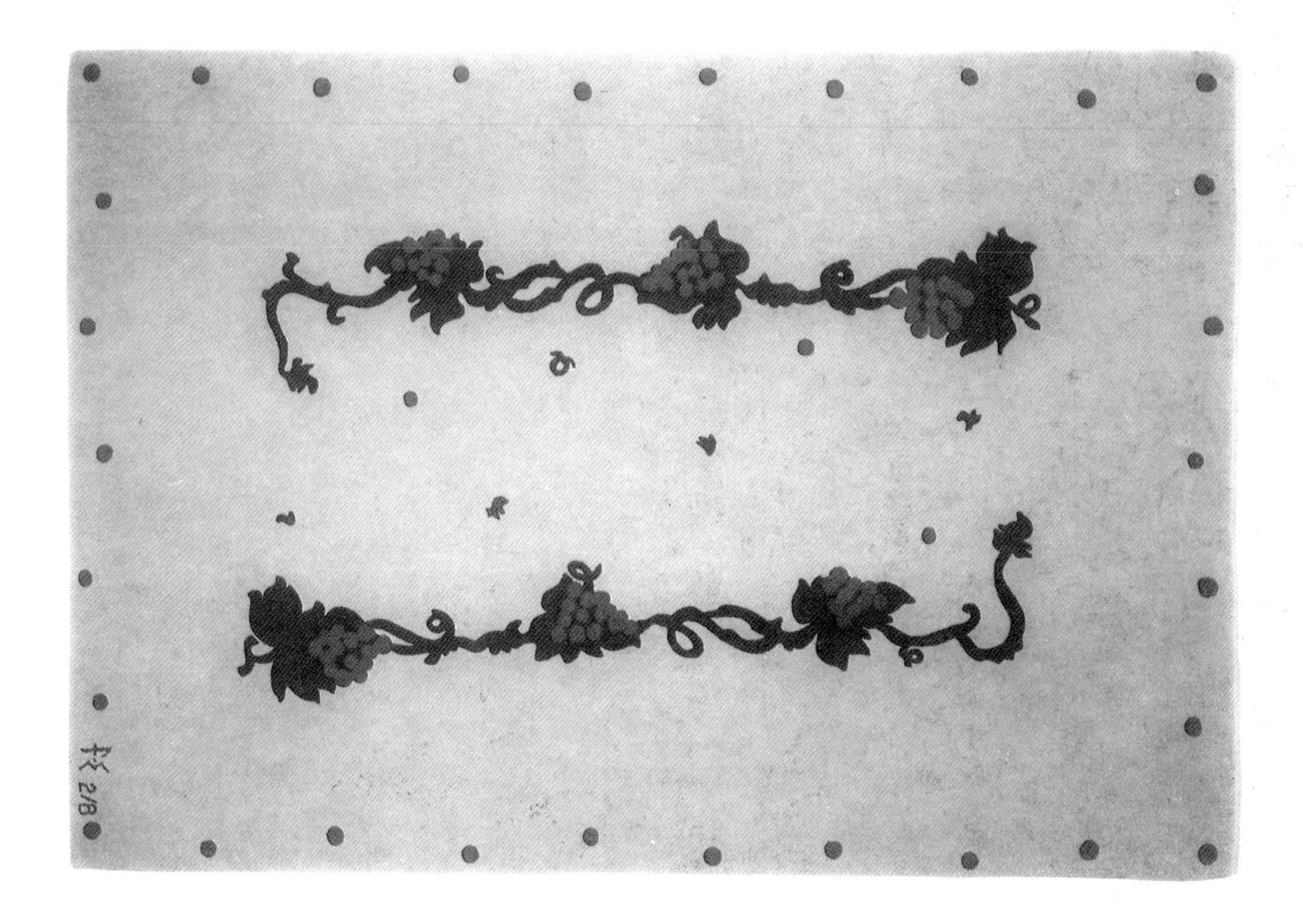

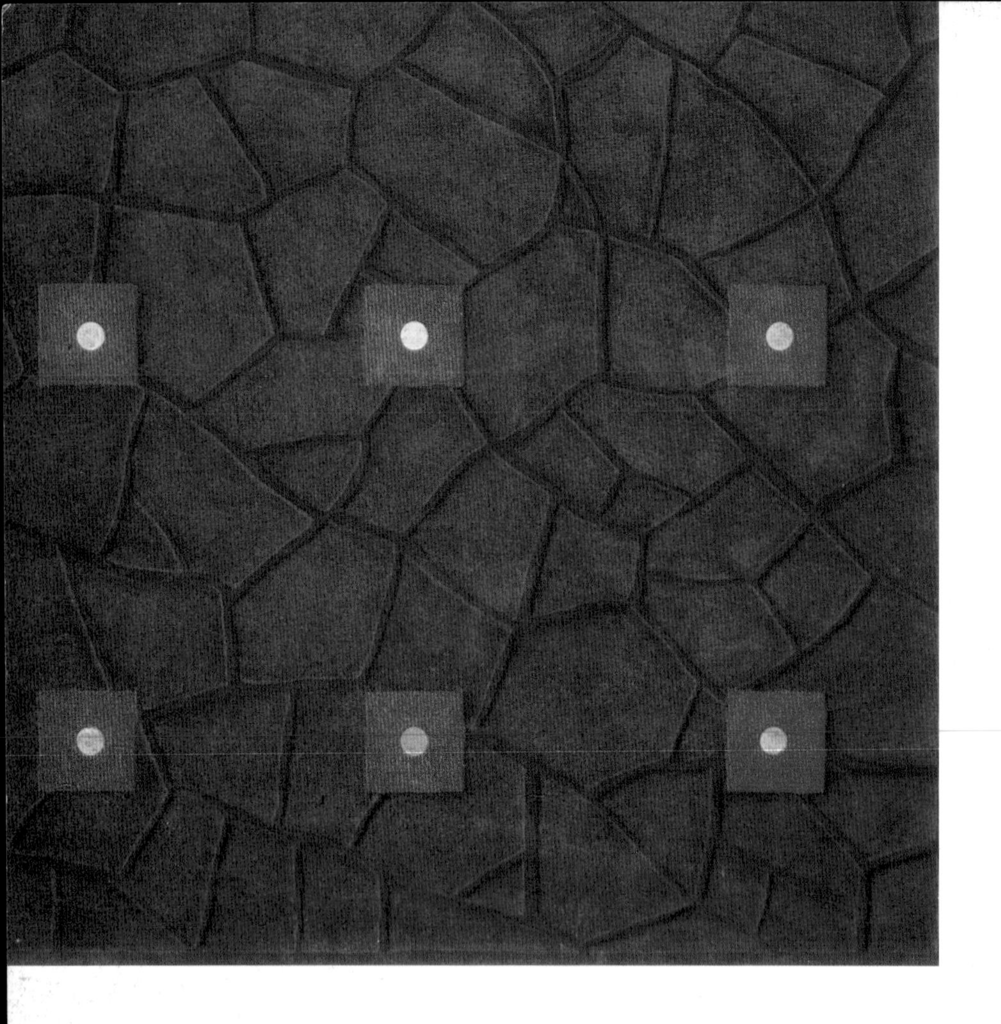

Left: Carpet (detail), Andrea Branzi, 1991, produced in a limited edition for Galerie Yves Gastou. Photograph courtesy of Galerie Yves Gastou.

Below: *Initiation* carpet, Sylvain Dubuison, 1991, produced in a limited edition for Galerie Yves Gastou. Photograph courtesy of Galerie Yves Gastou.

Opposite: *J. Greystoke* chairs, Alfredo Arribas, 1990, produced by Carlos Jane Camacho. Photograph courtesy of IDPA.

The legend of Tarzan, or Greystoke, presents the conflicts of nature and civilized life. Can the wild be confined within the supposedly civilized? Are the things which are exciting and alive in nature doomed to a slow death when brought inside and tamed? Greystoke is a legend of romance and heroism, and in romantic fiction, nature and the great outdoors were best left untouched by civilization. But man was always trying to reconstruct nature within his ordered environment. Romantic

Right: *J. Greystoke* chair, Alfredo Arribas, 1990, produced by Carlos Jane Camacho. Photograph courtesy of IDPA.

English gardens of the eighteenth century recreated the myth of nature and Greek follies in the countryside; Romantic paintings were full of nobility living the fantasy in pastoral settings. In Alfredo Arribas's chair *J. Greystoke* he presents the evolution from jungle to industrialized world through sensual forms that attempt to reinstate an animal nobility with man-made materials. Arribas describes the chair as "the accumulation of many generations. Her arms and legs are sinuous, similar to those which were often seen at the beginning of the century. The bottom is sturdy, postwar. The torso more modern and light, almost volatile. The waist very sculpted with technometal embellishments." Certainly, the chair back resembles elephant ears, with two tusks descending to support the chair. There is also an allusion to the work of Italian designer Carlo Mollino, evident in much of Arribas's furniture design; for example, the split seat and back appeared in Mollino's 1940 chair designed for Luisa and Luigi Licitra. Mollino was a designer for whom the human form held a fascination, even an eroticism which was radical for its time. Arribas is fascinated by the animal, although he has also designed with more human analogies. As Arribas tells the story of Greystoke, the animal can indeed be brought indoors without losing its power; in fact, it gains a new power through merging with design.

Arribas's *J. Greystoke* is produced by the Spanish furniture manufacturer Carlos Jane Camacho, which also produced the *Gaulino* chair and stool by Oscar Tusquets. Tusquets's collection is lighter and more sinewy than the Arribas chair, but still in an animalistic mode. Both Tusquets and Arribas are at the forefront of Spanish design, although their interests and sensibilities differ. Arribas, who is thirty-seven, is well known for his dramatic interiors for restaurants and clubs, such as the Velvet Bar, and the bar Torres de Avila in Barcelona, designed with Javier Mariscal. Tusquets, a half-generation older, is an architect and designer who has been influenced by the environs of his Catalan home. Nature is perhaps for Tusquets the use of that which exists about him, that which is real and particular to his environment. His *Gaulino* chair is true in material, natural wood, to the sources of his inspiration; it is neither an animated nor a true "faux" interpretation. Naturalism offers enough richness and inspiration to give the most divergent thinking a meeting place.

A renewed interest in nature, in its plant and animal and mineral forms, is manifest at the end of the twentieth century. The children of the sixties have grown up, and have an interest in saving the environment. In fashion, ecology and consumerism have come to make strange bedfellows. The same public that craves the new and the interesting is also concerned about where its favorite cosmetics, clothes, and objects come from, and where they will go after use. Although much design does not use natural materials (which would require killing a lot of trees), it has taken quickly to the preservation of the image of nature. By supplying the public with substitutes, things that look like nature, they show their often genuine concern for the fashionable world's loss of touch with nature.

Furniture designers have either literally returned to nature with their renewed interest in Primitivism and the making from raw materials, or have transposed the images of nature onto chairs, tables, and lights. Others began midway with domesticated nature, farm animals or the cultivated garden. In fact, many a designer at the turn of the twenty-first century is unfamiliar with wild and savage nature. This generation grew up in the cities or suburbs of Europe. They discovered nature through secondary sources: museums, zoos, and television. Through these same images they will reinstate nature into the modern habitat. Thus, the New Naturalism is the synthesis of all that is available to designers in terms of technology and the images and myths of nature. It is a synthesis intended for the enrichment of modern life.

Above and Right: *Gaulino* chairs and stool, Oscar Tusquets, 1990, manufactured by Carlos Jane Camacho. Photographs courtesy of IDPA.

Bricolage

The French word *bricoleur*, which refers to those who make things from whatever is available to them, has become the description of choice for many designers of lighting, decorative objects, and furniture. The designers of the group 18 Août call themselves "makers of objects"; others consider themselves inventors. These titles are a means to distinguish bricolage, the work of the Bricoleur, from that which reflects a superficial understanding of production. The term has credibility only if the designer enters the world of production. Whether the production involves the ancient craft of glass blowing or the latest technology of laser cutting, the designer working as artisan or alongside the artisan discovers the possibilities and the limits of ideas. It is this return to physical involvement in design, rather than blind faith in the superiority of mass assembly, that defines the Bricoleur in New Design.

Bricolage today involves a mix of "found" and produced materials. The Bricoleurs enjoy the search, the accumulation, the making, and the event of the final use and display; they have gone beyond society's need to amass objects to the actual act of generation. They have backgrounds solely as consumers as often as they are graduates of design schools. Often their experience is a combination of industrial design, sculpture, and interior design. It is the ability to see inspiration in everything that forms the being of contemporary society, from refuse to precious materials, that defines the Bricoleur. They are perhaps true Renaissance men, brought to full potential by the challenge of a world equally rich in new technologies and old throwaways.

Some designers had no choice but to create from what they found about them. In England, where a furniture industry that takes risks with new designers does not exist, designers had to create an industry for themselves. For some, the desire was simply to begin to make objects. By the mid-1980s, it was possible to make things with one's hands without being categorized as a craftsman or a latent hippie. Artists such as Tom Dixon began, with no design school background, to make objects out of salvage. Dixon, at that time with Creative Salvage, and others (André Dubreuil and Ron Arad) developed what would be the base of a London design community. Each worked alone and in a unique style, nurturing his own small furniture industry. By 1991, when four Englishmen—Tom Dixon, Ron Arad, Nigel Coates, and Jasper Morrison—made a big splash at the Milan furniture fair, the Bricoleur had reached the status of Designer.

Opposite: Salvaged-metal chair (detail), Tom Dixon, 1987, produced as a unique piece by the artist. Photograph courtesy of Tom Dixon.

Left: Cut sheet-metal chair, Tom Dixon, 1990, produced in a limited edition by the artist. Photograph courtesy of Tom Dixon.

Below: *Poltrona Bird* reclining chair, Tom Dixon, 1990, manufactured by Cappellini. Photograph courtesy of Cappellini.

Above: Salvaged-metal chairs, Tom Dixon, 1986, produced in a limited edition by the artist. Photograph courtesy of Tom Dixon.

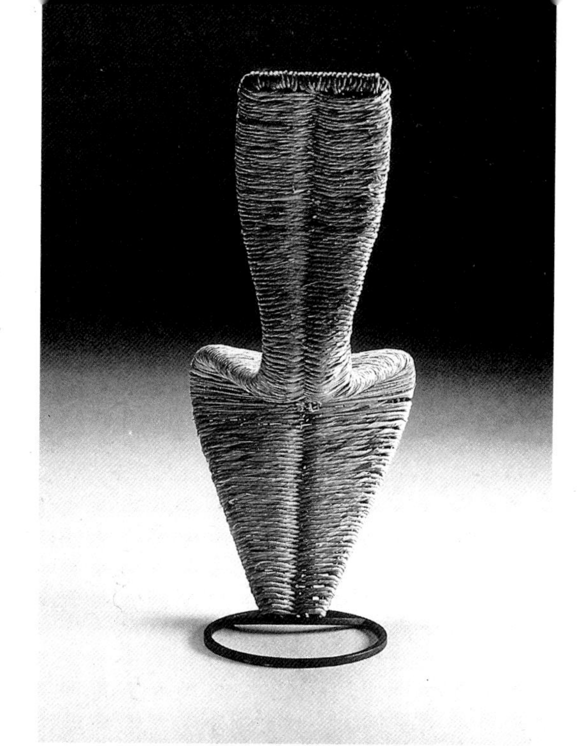

Left: *S* chair, Tom Dixon, 1986–87, manufactured by Cappellini since 1991. Photograph courtesy of Cappellini.

Below: *S* chair, Tom Dixon, 1986–87, produced by the artist. Photograph courtesy of Tom Dixon.

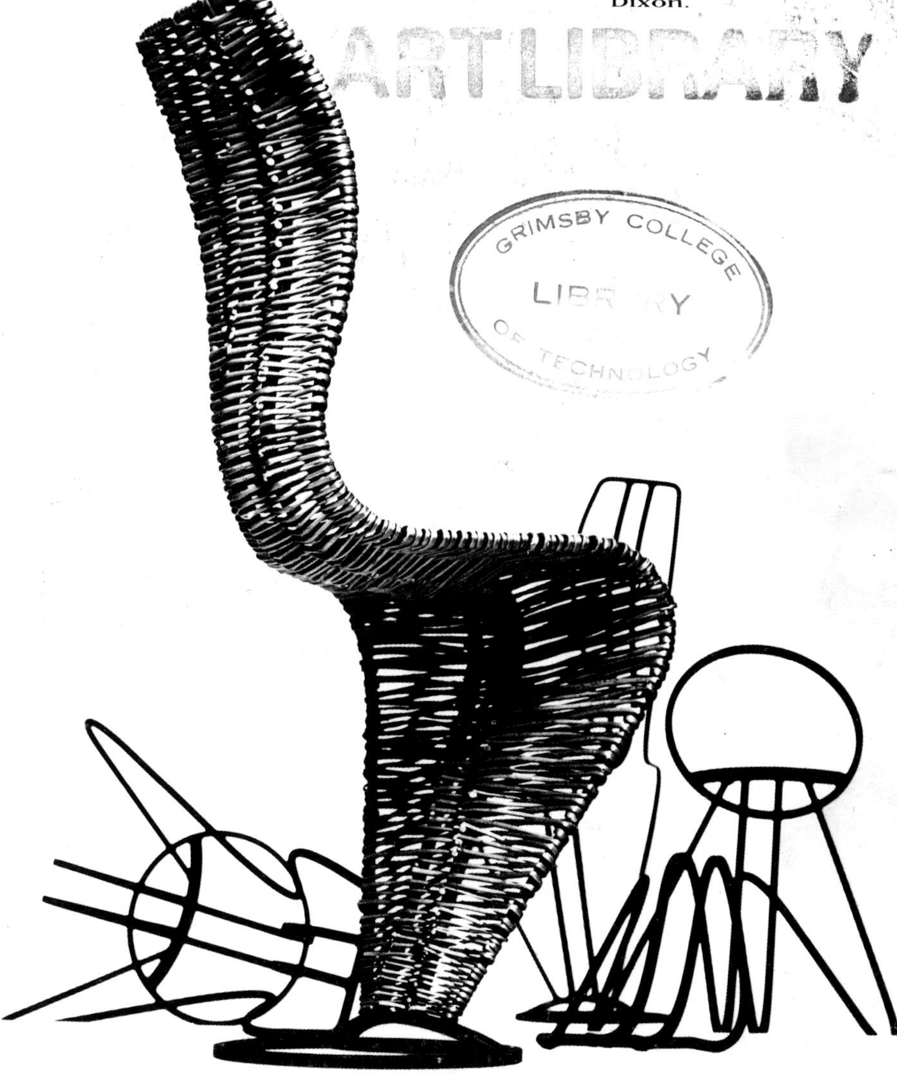

Salvage design and any odd mix of welded-metal furniture was never meant to be an end in itself. It was only a resource, a way to create when there were few other alternatives. For Tom Dixon, working in metal is still an important part of his work, but not his only medium. Dixon is interested in the potential of materials. Sometimes his acquisition of a new machine will spur a wave of new ideas and, therefore, forms. The results range from his gold chairs cut from flat sheets of metal to designs in mind for wood or even transparent materials.

Dixon's evolution has not occurred in isolation. His work has grown and diversified through his collaborations with a variety of people from all segments of the creative community, from Mick Jagger, for whom he designed background sets for videos, to architects such as Nigel Coates. He has worked on a number of designs with Coates, including an enormous clock on the exterior of a building in Japan called The Wall, and light fixtures for the Katharine Hamnett boutique in Glasgow. He is also working with the Italian manufacturer Cappellini on a series of metal chairs covered in rush; they are also producing his *S* chair and an upholstered piece called *Poltrona Bird*.

Above: Salvaged-metal chair, Tom Dixon, 1987, produced as a unique piece by the artist. Photograph courtesy of Tom Dixon.

Right: Wire chairs, Tom Dixon, 1991, produced in a limited edition by the artist. Photograph courtesy of Tom Dixon.

Opposite: Cut sheet-metal chair and tables, Tom Dixon, 1990, produced by the artist. Photograph courtesy of Tom Dixon.

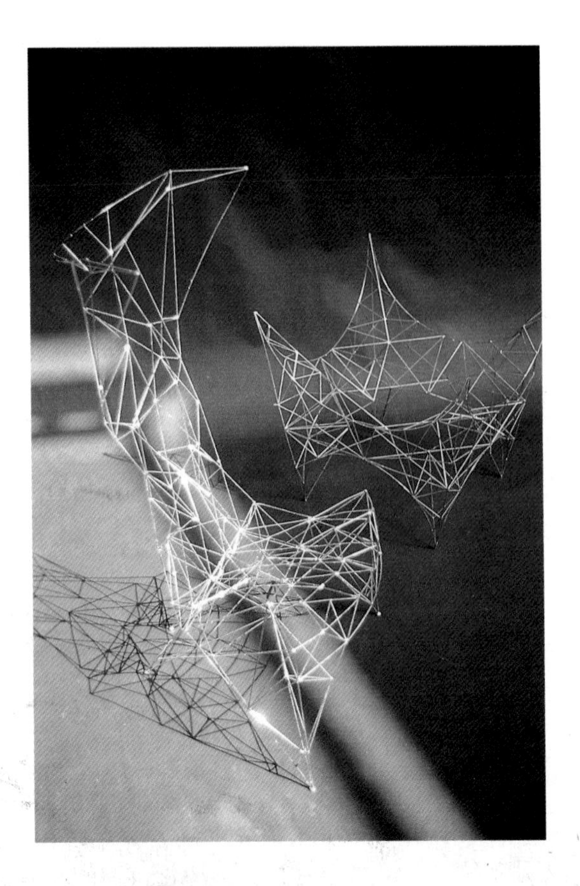

Dixon wants his work to be available to a broader public; he also wants to make money. Both of these factors have led him to Italy, where there is unquestionably a history of aggressive manufacturers willing to take risks. Yet, even with Cappellini, it is Dixon who has made the extra effort to find solutions for more economical production; to save on labor expenses, Dixon went to India to find the craftsmen to work on the rush seats. Like many of his generation born in the 1960s, Dixon has become an entrepreneur with a conscience. He is happy to see his designs touching a growing public and becoming less exclusive. Certainly, his furniture is found in galleries and in the private collections of the rich and famous, but the source of his one-of-a-kind pieces is his once-limited means. Now he can do it all. His London workshop is cluttered with ongoing projects, ranging from a one-of-a-kind chandelier for a London restaurant to prototypes for chair production in Italy. So many projects interest him. He still exudes a bit of his old club-kid charm and restlessness, with an offhanded manner that seems to say, "don't try to label me, or bore me, or tell me what I can and cannot do." To date, Dixon has been in bands, worked in clubs, designed furniture, had his work exhibited in major museums, and collaborated on designs for video and theater. These activities are entries into design that can teach the observant more about human needs, movement in space, communication, sensuality, and self-expression than any design-school education. In the New Design, form, proportion, and color are used to represent an active and physical relationship to space and emotion. Dixon's intuitive grasp of such expression has led him from a beginning as an artist, guided by his own unschooled eye, to his current place as a designer open to limitless temptations.

Left: *Party Furniture*, Tom Dixon, 1991, manufactured by Cappellini. Photograph courtesy of Cappellini.

Below: *Poltrona Fat* chairs, Tom Dixon, 1990, manufactured by Cappellini. Photograph courtesy of Cappellini.

Opposite: *Party Furniture* and chair, Tom Dixon, 1986, produced in a limited edition by the artist. Photograph courtesy of Tom Dixon.

Above: ***Heart & Industry*** **chair, Ron Arad, 1990, produced by One-Off Ltd. Photograph courtesy of One-Off.**

Ron Arad is another designer whose name immediately invokes images of metal furniture and reappropriated materials, but Arad is not easily categorized. With his company One-Off, he has created a self-contained workshop that designs, builds, distributes, exhibits, and works in association with Ron Arad the architect. One such architecture project (with C. Norton and S. McAdam) is the interior of the public spaces of the new Tel Aviv Opera House. However, the energies within the studio influence each other; there is a traceable continuum to the work. One piece grows from the last. A shape left open in one design comes to a complete closure in the next. In this approach, Arad says, "the ideas and the influences come from within"; from within the group, and certainly from within Arad's imagination. One-Off, writes Arad, "is constantly speeding through ideas, sometimes merely noting them by a crude artifact, sometimes processing them to a greater degree. The more refined and laboured a design becomes, the more it is in danger of losing its original raison d'être."[11]

In his *Spring* collection for Moroso, many of the forms Arad first worked with in welded steel, such as *Volume 2 for 2,* have been reinterpreted into soft upholstered forms. "They are," says Arad, "all part of the same family." Working in the foam that covers the metal structure, cutting the shapes, and playing with ideas of empty and full, soft and hard, light and heavy, are new facets of a design evolution. Working with Moroso has been a means to bring his designs to a wider audience. For, as much as the designs of the Bricoleur can be conceived and developed within the studio, a chair like *No Spring Chicken* can be reproduced far more efficiently in the big factory. Of course, appropriating existing resources is one of the talents of the Bricoleur.

Much of the Moroso collection is an extension of Arad's interest in movement. Chairs that lean forward when not in use will roll back as you sit in them to support your weight comfortably. The Moroso chair *Big Heart* is modeled after the original metal chair *Heart & Industry,* a heart of polished stainless steel with just enough of an indentation at its widest part to create a seat. The tip of the heart is weighted, so that it rises to a vertical and more apparent "heart" orientation when not in use. For *Looming Lloyd,* leaded stainless steel shoes can be clamped onto any chair with four legs; the shoes throw it forward, making it apparently ready to walk away. Even in Arad's wood furniture, like the *Split Table,* movement is part of the design; the table can be stretched to twice its length by simply pulling at either end and letting the wood ribs slide apart. Other pieces—chairs that split to form two chairs, chairs that roll, seats that bounce—are all part of Arad's various experiments and obvious sense of humor.

Ron Arad has often been called an artist; he says he is an architect. Looking at his new Chalk

Opposite, top: ***Three Thirds of a Table*** **welded-steel table, Ron Arad, 1989, produced by One-Off Ltd. Photograph courtesy of One-Off.**

Opposite, bottom: ***Double Rietveld*** **chair, Ron Arad, 1991, produced by One-Off Ltd. Photograph courtesy of One-Off.**

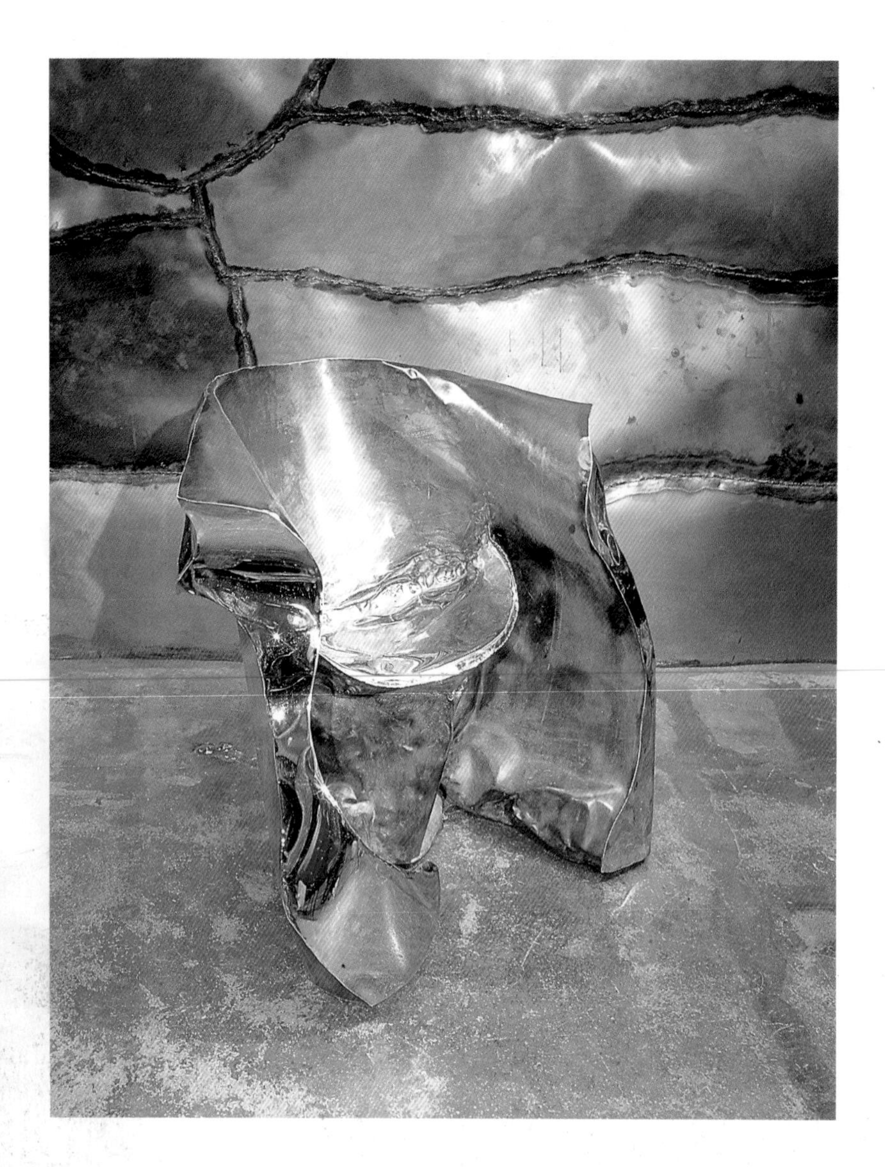

Road studio (and One-Off headquarters) in London, where a transparent ceiling of wire mesh and plastic is supported by large, curving, cut-metal shapes, one sees forms that are sculpture, but also, indeed, architecture. The fact that he enhances a structural necessity, or creates his own structural elements, is less derivative of a desire to create art than it is of Arad's constant affirmation that one creates something out of everything. Every part of the studio has been created, touched, and worked on by One-Off in an integral architectural assemblage. There is no division of duty.

Left: ***Italian Fish*** **metal chair, Ron Arad, 1988, produced by One-Off Ltd. Photograph courtesy of One-Off.**

Below: ***Little Heavy*** **and** ***Big Easy Volume*** **chairs, Ron Arad, 1989, produced by One-Off Ltd. Photograph courtesy of One-Off.**

Right: *Eight by One* metal chairs, Ron Arad, 1991, produced by One-Off Ltd. Photograph courtesy of One-Off.

Below: *Strict Family* metal chairs, Ron Arad, 1991, produced by One-Off Ltd. Photograph courtesy of One-Off.

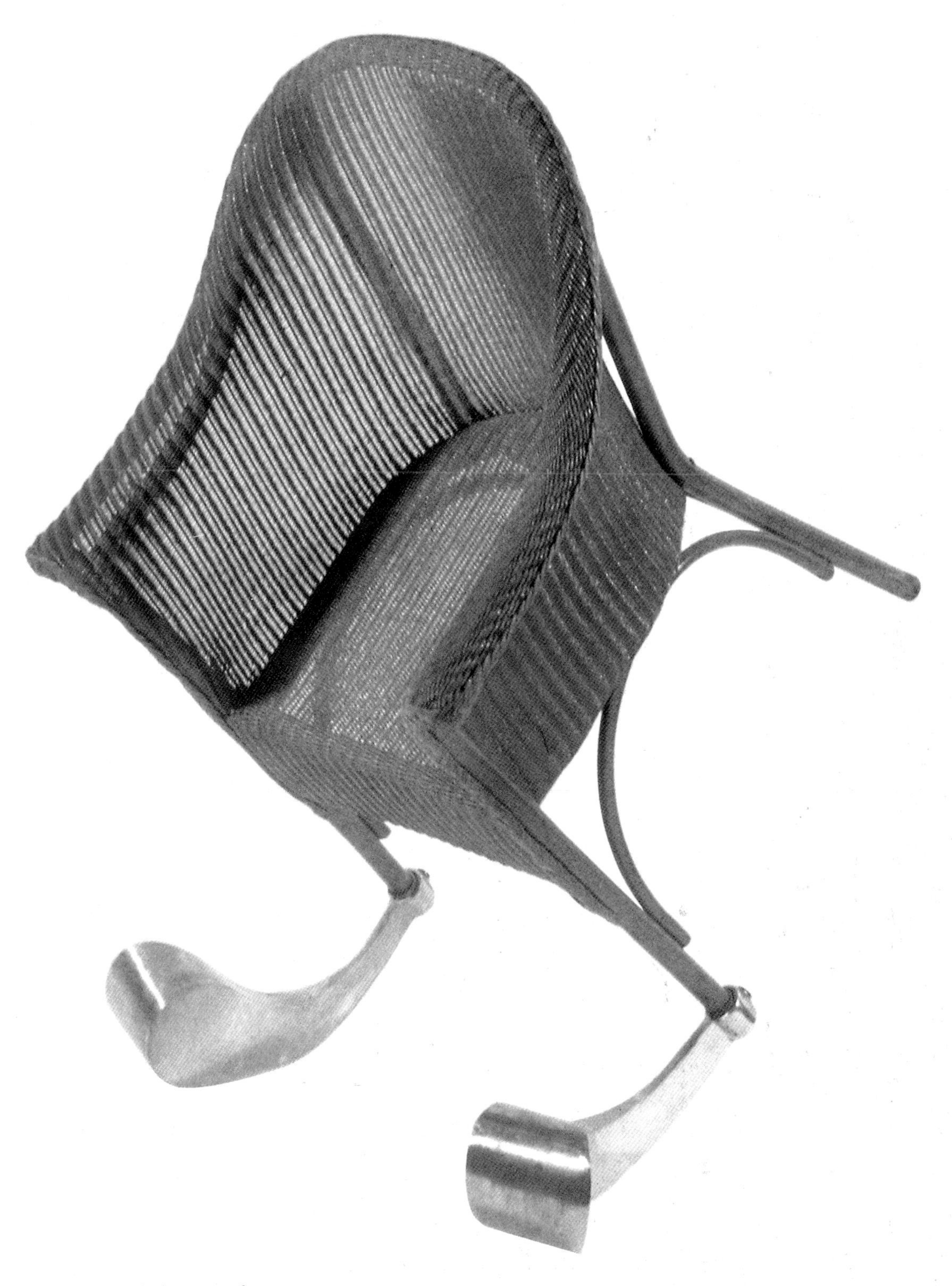

Above: *Looming Lloyd* chair with weighted shoes, Ron Arad, 1990, produced by One-Off Ltd. Photograph courtesy of One-Off.

Opposite: One-Off studio (detail), London, designed by Ron Arad, 1991. Photograph courtesy of One-Off.

Opposite: *Low Tilt* armchair from the *Spring* collection, Ron Arad, 1991, manufactured by Moroso, Photograph courtesy of Moroso.

Right: *No Spring Chicken* chair from the *Spring* collection, Ron Arad, 1991, manufactured by Moroso. Photograph courtesy of Moroso.

Below: *Chair By Its Cover* chairs, Ron Arad, 1989—90, produced by One-Off Ltd. Photograph courtesy of One-Off.

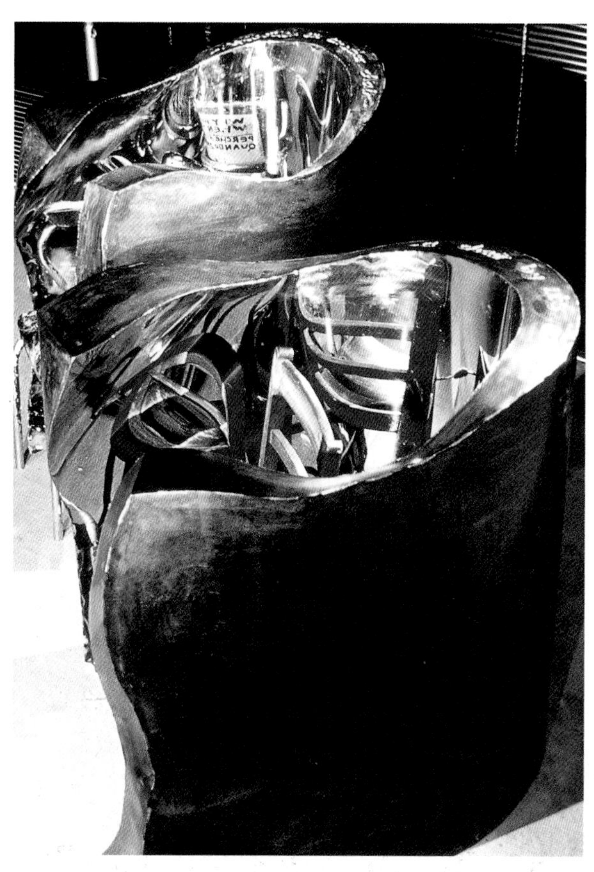

Many young designers have followed this example of creating an all-inclusive studio. In Paris, the three-man design team of 18 Août now concentrates on the small object and the lamp. In 1987, at an average age of twenty-four, they began to explore new technologies. In order to ensure that their designs are realized and to maintain control of their creations, Fabrice Berrux, Bruno Moretti, and Pascal Oriol became not only the designers but the production chiefs, distributors, and promoters of their work. Their intent is to bring their work to the widest public possible, which they can do only with an understanding and control of the process of invention and consumption. Their work is now distributed under the mark Dix Heures Dix, or 10.10, a company located within the same ancient workshop in eastern Paris as 18 Août; it is all the same family.

An important early design of 18 Août is the hot plate *Chaud/Froid* (hot/cold), which expresses the succinctness of their ideas in interlocking spirals of matte and polished chromed steel. Their designs are smart yet simple. They are also full of metaphors, an element which makes the user think twice about his relationship to the object before him. A giant laser-cut flower becomes a vase; a wrapped piece of fiberglass bearing the inscription PS 27, for Psalm 27, which reads, "the eternal is my light and my salvation," becomes a lamp. The raised letters on an engraved glass ashtray tell us the dictionary definition of, of course, an ashtray. Recent designs include a garbage can in the guise of a bomb. These are the products of three unjaded minds.

While 18 Août do not salvage materials with which to begin their work, they have had to search out and adapt available and generally inexpensive technologies to give form to their creations. They have chosen to design small objects with the resourcefulness of industrial appropriators rather

Opposite: *Oui-Oui* hand-blown glass lamps with resin base and pompon switch, 18 Août, 1990, produced for 10.10. Photograph by Jean-Marc Tingaud.

Below: *Chaud/Froid* (hot/cold) polished and matte chromed-steel hot plate, 18 Août, 1983, produced for 10.10. Photograph by Jean-Marc Tingaud.

than industrial designers. On a wall vase the word *fleurs* is engraved on a flat brass plaque as one would engrave a club trophy, or in this case a grave marker. The laser-cut flower face for the vase uses a technology that can quickly cut out almost any two-dimensional shape from flat metal sheets, a technology being used more and more in thin metal chairs and tables. At 18 Août, the cut-out flowers are attached to their stalk-vessels in what resembles a factory assembly line. Here, however, the workers are young design school students, who are more than eager to get hands-on experience in design production.

Above: *Poussah* chromed-metal and bakelized-paper lamp, 18 Août, 1987, produced for 10.10. Photograph by Jean-Marc Tingaud.

Right: Chromed-brass wall vase, 18 Août, 1990, produced for 10.10. Photograph courtesy of 10.10.

Opposite: *Sol/Sol* garbage can, 18 Août, 1990, produced for 10.10. Photograph courtesy of 10.10.

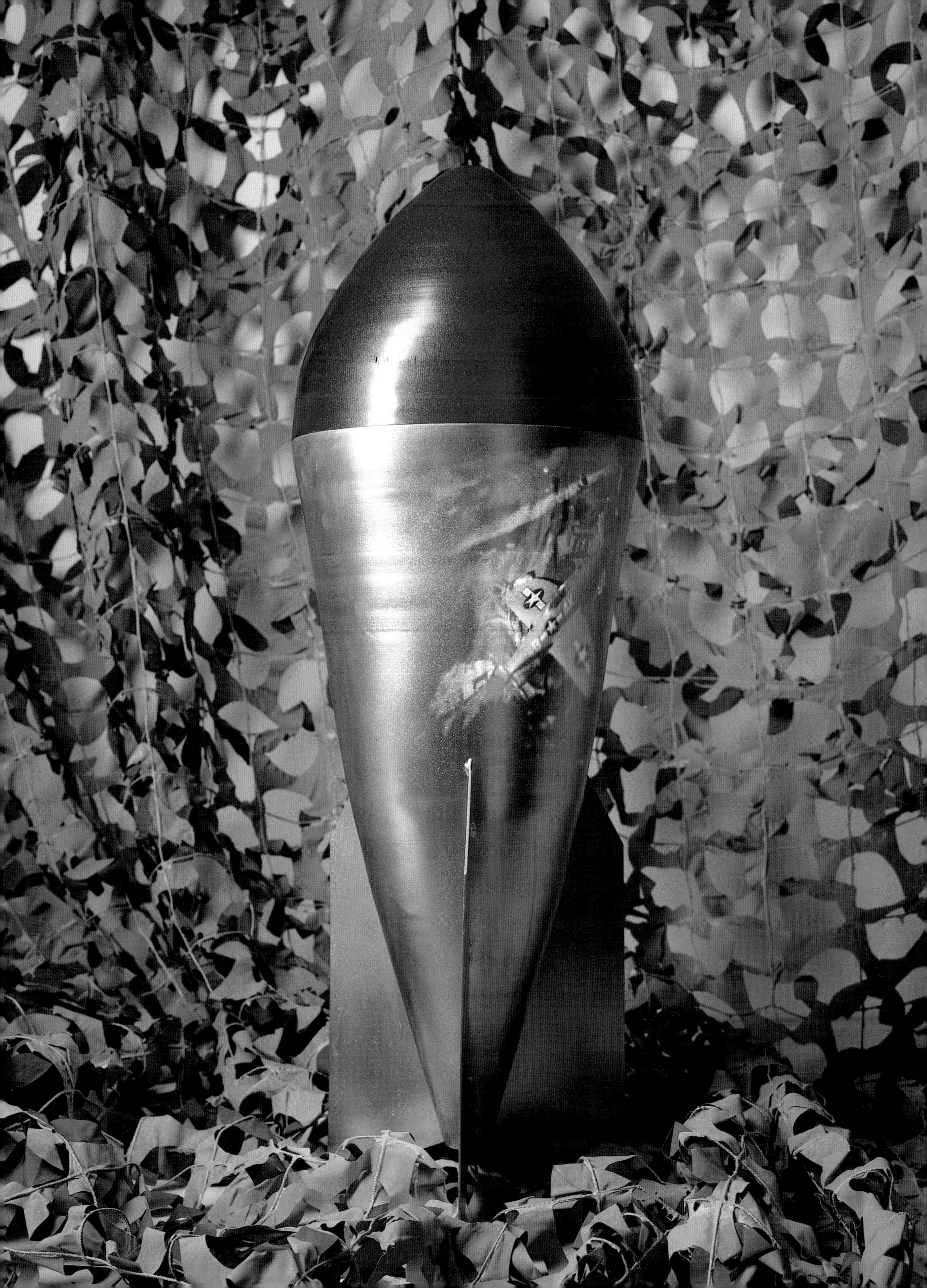

Above right: *Ziggourat* white PVC lamp, 18 Août, 1990, produced for 10.10. Photograph by Jean-Marc Tingaud.

Opposite: *PS 27* lamp, 18 Août, 1989, produced for 10.10. Photograph courtesy of 10.10.

Above: *Scoubidou* nickel-plated fruit bowl, 18 Août, 1989, produced for 10.10. Photograph by Jean-Marc Tingaud.

Opposite: *Navaronne* vase, 18 Août, 1990, produced for 10.10. Photograph by Jean-Marc Tingaud.

Above: *Flower* polished-aluminum vases, 18 Août, 1989, produced for 10.10. Photograph by Jean-Marc Tingaud.

Right: *Flower* polished-aluminum vases, 18 Août, 1989, produced for 10.10. Photograph courtesy of 10.10.

Opposite: *N.D.* table mirror with gold-tinted, stainless-steel "tresses" forming stand, 18 Août, 1990, produced for 10.10. Photograph by Jean-Marc Tingaud.

Another Bricoleur, one whose work is closer in spirit to that of an artist, was the late Marco de Gueltzl, who worked in Paris. Employing glass, soldered steel, and junkyard metals, de Gueltzl worked fast and furiously, with no time for dogma. Certainly the broken glass pieces which he let grow in form as he worked were not adaptable to mass production; nor were they meant to be. Yet he did design several chairs and more formal pieces which could be duplicated in limited series. One, the upholstered *St. Petersburg* chair, bears scant resemblance to his earlier work (no globs of soldered steel) except for his trademark green glass, wrapped in metal at each arm. This very baroque-styled chair has a quick, "fashion-of-the-times" look; others, such as the chair of steel tubes or the buffet, seem somehow a more honest outgrowth of the struggle between art and production.

Above: Console, Marco de Gueltzl, 1989, produced in a limited edition by the artist. Photograph courtesy of VIA.

Right: *Dagobert* chair, Marco de Gueltzl, 1989, produced in a limited edition by the artist. Photograph courtesy of VIA.

Above: Steel tube chair, Marco de Gueltzl, 1990, produced in a limited edition by the artist. Photograph courtesy of VIA.

De Gueltzl was in the realm of the Bricoleur/Artist without the aspirations for mass production. His work is collected, traded at auction, and very expensive. He represented the growing market of design that permits exclusivity. This exclusivity is in great contrast to the works of Marcel Breuer and others, which became exclusive but were designed for the public. Breuer's chairs eventually became the property of the public at large; they could be because they were conceived of for widespread production. It is difficult to imagine the same outcome for a de Gueltzl; a flooded market would certainly not be the desire of those who purchase his work as "antiques of the future." First, if he chooses, the Bricoleur must make a move towards not just the "found," but the reproducible as well; then he will be a designer and not an artist.

Above: Armoire, Marco de Gueltzl, 1990, produced in a limited edition by the artist. Photograph courtesy of VIA.

Left: Candelabra, Marco de Gueltzl, 1990, produced in a limited edition by the artist. Photograph courtesy of VIA.

Opposite: *St. Petersburg* chair, Marco de Gueltzl, 1990, produced in a limited edition by the artist. Photograph courtesy of VIA.

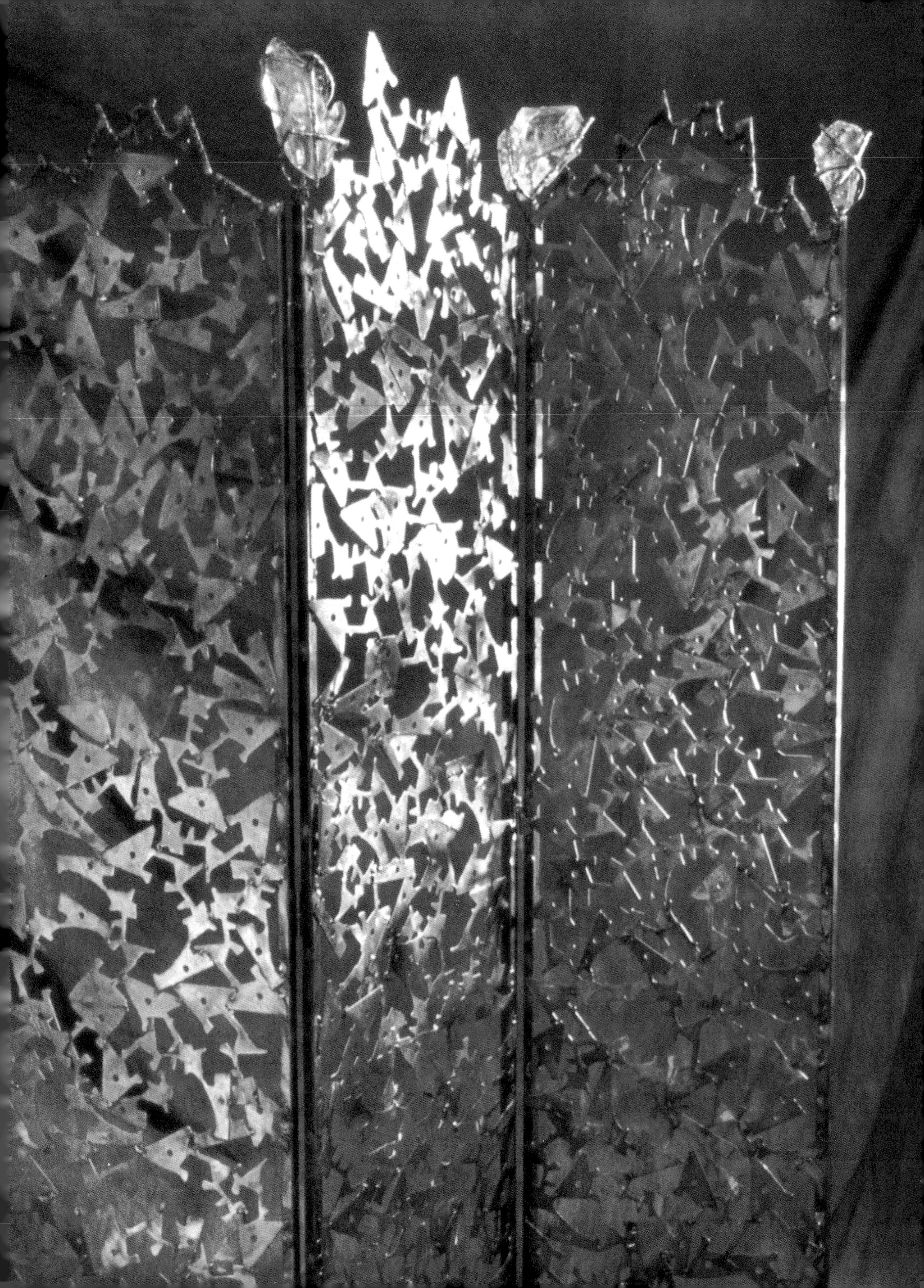

Above: Sand-blasted table with steel tube and welded-metal chairs, Marco de Gueltzl, 1990, produced in a limited edition by the artist. Photograph courtesy of VIA.

Right: Console tree, Marco de Gueltzl, 1990, produced in a limited edition by the artist. Photograph courtesy of VIA.

Opposite: Folding screen (detail), Marco de Gueltzl, 1989, produced in a limited edition by the artist. Photograph courtesy of VIA.

The New Modern

The word *modern* has taken on so many meanings since the nineteenth century that today it is almost without meaning. Here, using it to mean of one's time, as did Manet, one can begin to investigate the design of the present. We must first note that the present is highly eclectic. Those who are modern are often without words to describe their work, which is involved in events, passing moments, sentiment, and rigor. It is work that might fit into other categories within this book (such as The New Baroque or Bricolage, which are here also called modern), but it also crosses into new areas, such as bolidism or mysticism. However, in the eclecticism which marks the design world now, there are those whose work crosses all lines and still remains clear, somehow unencumbered by what some would call chaos. For the modernist today, chaos is the norm. The New Moderns, and in many ways all of the designers in this book, are difficult to classify. Fortunately, the visual is not limited by any lack of explanatory vocabulary.

Borek Sípek personifies the unknown in design. More than anyone else, he brought the regard of the object to a level of mysticism that completely breaks with the rationality of the Western European masters. Eastern European by birth, Sípek comes to design with a mistrust of the truth, a subjugation of the master to the work, a tradition of doubt and spirituality. "The most important factor in contemporary design," says Sípek, "is not that it is attractive, but that it relates to the individual. As to those who consider functionality the most important element, I can tell them now that they remain in the most primitive stage of their design development."[12] To which individual must the designer relate, and how? Each designer must answer this question for himself. Designs, therefore, become autobiographical, based on an individual embodying the memories, desires, manner of living, and even an idealized physical transposition with the author/designer.

Who then is Borek Sípek? As complex as most, his past has crossed the borders of a changing Europe. Sípek left Czechoslovakia as a young man; after a passage through Germany, he settled in Amsterdam. He is an architect, designer, father, teacher, and someone who muses over issues such as illusion, spirituality, and opportunism. He is also an extremely prolific designer.

Sípek's work in furniture, objects, and interiors reflects diverse influences, which, in Sípek's words, "make it harder to choose." Perhaps it is because of this that he chooses an abstract vision of the world, an abstraction which results, by his own definition, in a "non-abstract" object, in fact innumerable objects. Sípek's output is prodigious. There are his multicolored rattan chairs for Driade which curve in hornlike shapes, and for Driade Follies, a collection of glassware which seemed unprecedented in its inventiveness, elegance, and detail: Lacy crystal skirts encircle his wine glasses; a golden vine wraps his vase. His every variation was a sign that modern designers had underestimated the potential of the decorative object. Sípek went on to work in porcelain with Sèvres and Neotu. In his rediscovery of this traditional material, he developed a far from traditional vocabulary. Sípek supports his

Opposite: *Plana 18* benches from the *Dinamic* collection (detail), Massimo Iosa Ghini, 1987, manufactured by Moroso. Photograph courtesy of Moroso.

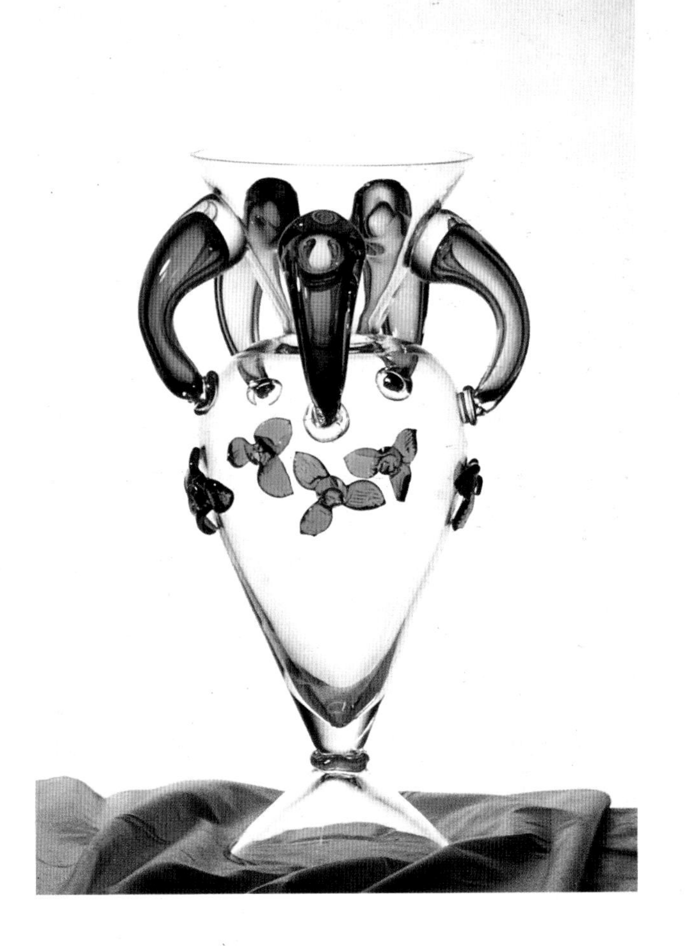

Below: Glass vase, Borek Sípek, 1990 produced for Neotu. Photograph courtesy of Neotu.

porcelain bowls on thick, spikelike protrusions—a shape he uses often, but which rarely seems aggressive. He mixes his own details with traditional fragments, as in the piece with a massive cut-glass collar that supports a vase on the diagonal. Sípek's work has an ability to surprise; it is joyous and layered with a collection of memories from across Europe.

When Sípek is designing objects and even furniture, he is, he says, "working for himself." This is his luxury and his challenge. The result is a design inseparable from himself. However, Sípek is increasingly drawn towards interior and architectural projects. He thinks architecture is more abstract, less tangible design, one which is tied into the needs of other people. In his design for the Shoebaloo shoe shop in Amsterdam, Sípek incorporates both his furniture designs and his understanding of the subtleties of color, light, and pattern. He treats light both as an abstract quality and as pattern, evidence of its existence.

Sípek has produced a collection of glassware for the Italian company Sawaya & Moroni. William Sawaya and Paolo Moroni have been collaborating with designers since 1984. Almost every one of the designs of their company has stood as a marker of up-to-the-minute modernity. They have produced the furniture of American architect and eminent postmodernist Michael Graves, and a collection by Englishman Charles Jencks, an architecture critic whose books have defined the postmodern movement and all stages of modernity to follow. They have worked with Ron Arad on his *Crust* chair, and, most recently, with Luigi Serafini and Marco Mencacci. They are in search of the modern, the standards of the moment, and not any particular style. "It is not," says Moroni, "important to reinvent, but to be inspired by your time."

Above: *Prorok* chair, Borek Sípek, 1988, manufactured by Driade. Photograph by Tom Vack.

Opposite: *Helena* chairs, Borek Sípek, 1988, manufactured by Driade. Photograph by Tom Vack.

Right: *Satomi San* table, Borek Sípek, 1988, produced in a limited edition for Neotu. Photograph courtesy of Neotu.

Above: *Bambi* chair, Borek Sípek, 1988, produced in a limited edition for Neotu. Photograph courtesy of Neotu.

Right, top: *Swann* tea service, Borek Sipek, 1988, manufactured by Driade Follies. Photograph by Leo Torri.

Right, bottom: *Anebo Tak* chair, Borek Sipek, 1987, manufactured by Driade. Photograph by Aldo Ballo.

Below: *Marcel* candlestick, Borek Sipek, 1988, manufactured by Driade Follies. Photograph by Leo Torri.

Above and Right: *Albertine* china collection, Borek Sipek, 1988, manufactured by Driade Follies. Photographs by Leo Torri.

Above: *Enrico* glassware collection, Borek Sípek, 1988, manufactured by Driade Follies. Photograph by Leo Torri.

Above: Glassware collection, Borek Sípek, 1990, produced by Sawaya & Moroni. Photograph courtesy of Sawaya & Moroni.

Right: *Luigi I* and *Luigi II* chandelier and lamp, Borek Sípek, 1988, manufactured by Driade Follies. Photograph by Leo Torri.

Above: Shoebaloo shoe shop, Amsterdam, furniture and interior design by Borek Sípek, 1991. Photograph courtesy of Borek Sipek.

Above: *Xaver* chair, William K. Sawaya, 1988, produced by Sawaya & Moroni. Photograph courtesy of Sawaya & Moroni.

Opposite: *Diva* chair, William K. Sawaya, 1987, produced by Sawaya & Moroni. Photograph courtesy of Sawaya & Moroni.

Sawaya and Moroni have observed changes in the design world through their own production and by witnessing a change in priorities of the young designers who regularly present their work to the company. Young designers have never before found it so easy to see their designs produced, since a growing number of furniture manufacturers are looking for new talent. The popularity of the designer today has resulted in a situation in which young designers show their press book and not their new ideas or drawings when they look for work. During this current deluge of design, young designers find fast, and often short-lived, success; "the life span of the designer has dropped from five

Left: *Santa* chair, Luigi Serafini, 1990, produced by Sawaya & Moroni. Photograph courtesy of Sawaya & Moroni.

Below: *La Belle* chair, William K. Sawaya, 1990, produced by Sawaya & Moroni. Photograph courtesy of Sawaya & Moroni.

Opposite: *Suspiral* chairs, Luigi Serafini, 1989, produced by Sawaya & Moroni. Photograph courtesy of Sawaya & Moroni.

Above: *Crust* chairs, Ron Arad, 1988, produced by Sawaya & Moroni. Photograph courtesy of Sawaya & Moroni.

to two or three years." Only a few, reflect Sawaya and Moroni, "will have the staying power." They use Starck as an example of someone who has lasted and who will continue to last, but they too have put together an impressive list of important designers and designs, which might well endure, but which, more important, have marked their time.

The importance of Sawaya & Moroni is their realistic and refreshing response to modern design as a time-event phenomenon. They accept as a basic premise that "what is modern" is always changing. They also understand that not all of design, even at its most conscientious and professional levels, will endure, and that it need not. They might not accept as "designers" those who have no design or even architectural background. Sawaya, himself a furniture designer, believes in the distinct domains of the artist, the designer, and the architect.

"All designers," he says, "know how to manipulate form and color to be in fashion, but at this point design loses its first function. You must know the rules [of each domain]." Sawaya's designs are decidedly in the domain of the designer, controlled and alive at the same time. Animated with minimal but direct gestures, they include the feminine *La Belle* and *Diva,* and the masculine *Xaver* with its arched metal spike fixing it firmly to the earth. There is also *La Bête,* which is far from stupid with its sweeping chrome structure pulling up the wooden seat. Sawaya's designs form the foundation of the company.

One of the designers currently working with Sawaya & Moroni is Luigi Serafini, a young Italian designer who flirted with the borders of the New Baroque in his *Suspiral* chair. The *Suspiral,* with its balance of simplicity and provocation, was one of the first designs out of Italy to employ curves, elegant upholstery in its buttoned seat, and twisted metal front legs which are reminiscent of garden furniture. Though still a restrained design, the *Suspiral* is evidence of the move towards greater animation and texture in Italian design. Serafini's later *Santa* chair goes even further by creating a humorous characterization, and thus narrative, in a design that is as minimal in line as it is full of animated spirit. This ability to animate the object, to open it out of pure function and into fiction, is what makes Serafini a New Modernist.

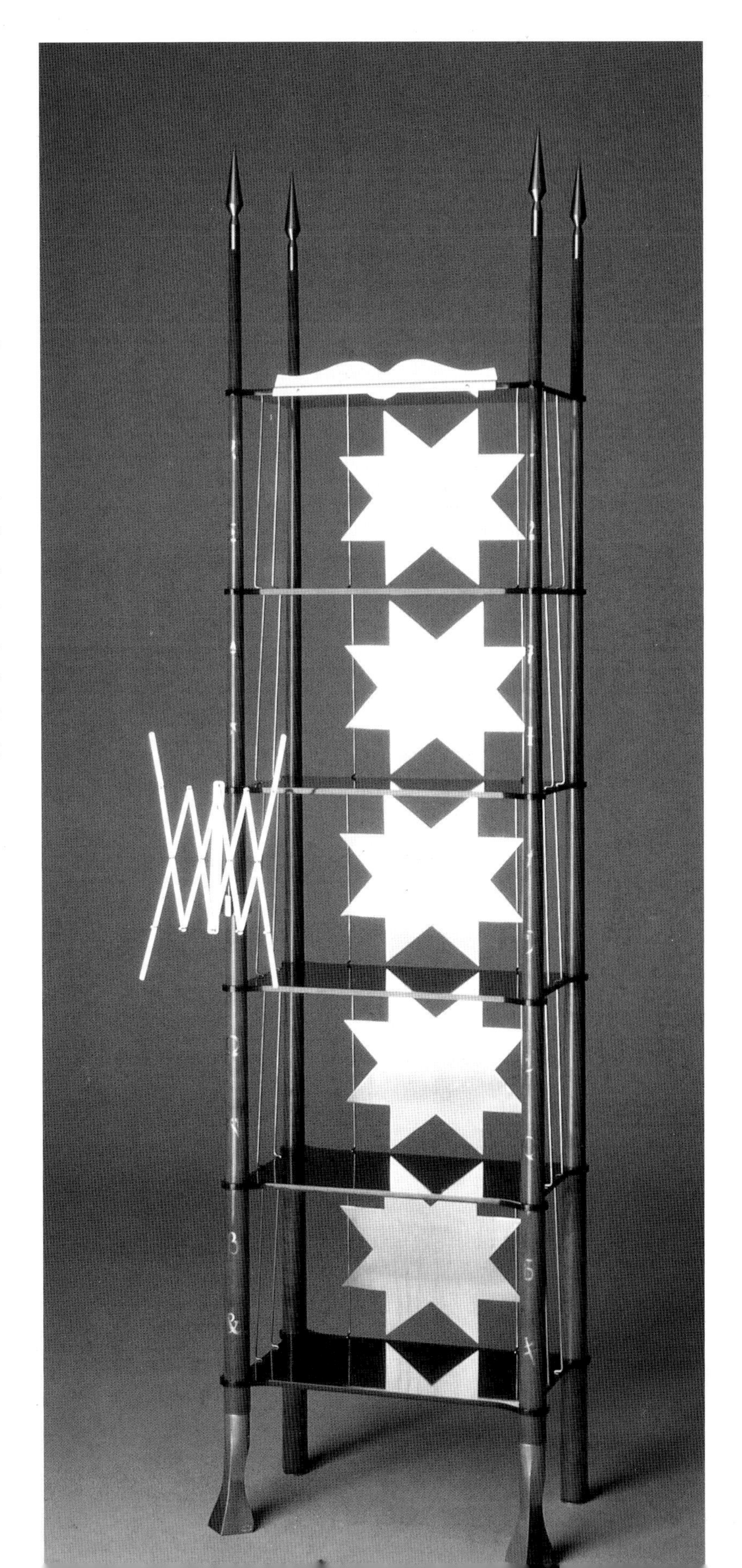

Right: *Libabel* bookcase, Jeannot Cerutti, 1989, produced by Sawaya & Moroni. Photograph courtesy of Sawaya & Moroni.

Below: *Bir Bin Besh* tables, Marco Mencacci, 1990, produced by Sawaya & Moroni. Photograph courtesy of Sawaya & Moroni.

Above: *Plana 18* benches from the *Dinamic* collection, Massimo Iosa Ghini, 1987, manufactured by Moroso. Photograph courtesy of Moroso.

The designs of Jeannot Cerutti and Marco Mencacci can also be considered New Modern. Cerutti's *Libabel* bookcase is decorated in stainless steel stars, spearheads, an accordion-fold arm, and wood supports, themselves covered with Greek and Roman letters and other symbols. *Libabel* is a modern warrior, aided by a bit of mysticism. Mencacci's *Tatlim* chair and *Bir Bin Besh* table are, on the other hand, domesticated modern. The *Tatlim* mixes the hard line of rational design with the sentiment of the doily, traditionally found in the "undesigned" home. *Bir Bin Besh* is a geometrized little wooden side table, to which is added a lamp with a diminutive lampshade. Each of these designs gives the impression that the designer has been playing in his parents' house, adding to the homey decor with pieces from his own make-believe world. These young Italian designers are inspired by comfortable memories from the 1950s and 1960s, translated by a design education and worldly experience into solutions for the 1990s.

Other young Italian designers are literally taking off, in a direction called bolidism, with Massimo Iosa Ghini in the forefront. Bolidism, as its name implies, is brash and dynamic design. Bolidists have often been called futuristic because of their preference for aerodynamic shapes and George Jetson cartoon colors. Yet this furniture is not for the future but the present. It is designed for the sector of the population that lives in the fast lane, on the highway, in the airport. It is young and it is "now," in the pop, cool sense of the word.

Massimo Iosa Ghini is right out of the television generation. In fact, he has worked in the world of television, designing sets. He is fascinated by computer design, electricity, and high-speed thinking. He has even been a cartoonist, so his furniture is not that unlikely an outgrowth of his multiple talents. His designs are not just bold, they seem to dominate the space they inhabit. Each seems to

command a certain distance from the neighboring stationary objects. The *Boomerang* sofa looks as though it will blast off at any minute. Flash Gordon? No, that would be someone looking at the future through the past. This is, instead, the work of a person who conceives of forms in three dimensions and gives each a sense of freedom.

Massimo Iosa Ghini's first collection, *New Tone* for Moroso, was a turning point, not just for Iosa Ghini, but for Moroso as well. It was the manufacturer's entry into high-profile furniture design, star designers, and the cutting edge. The collection was presented to great acclaim at the 1989 Milan Furniture Fair, when Iosa Ghini was thirty years old. Moroso has gone on to create a collection with Ron Arad, and Iosa Ghini has gone on and on. He designed several pieces for Memphis, which stood out strongly from the patterned works of Sottsass. For Lisar, a manufacturer of custom furniture, he created a collection of wood furniture of uncommon fluidity and craftsmanship in 1991; Iosa Ghini's one stipulation was that he would work entirely in wood. The result of the collaboration is a collection of twelve curved and twisted pieces which stretch the limits of the wood. The large-scale pieces will be repeated no more then ten times. While the Lisar collections represent Iosa Ghini at a new height of artistic and technical virtuosity, his collection of sunglasses for Silhouette shows his humorous and fashion-conscious side. The sunglasses and case are unmistakable bolidist ware, sleek and eye-catching. Each design is a limited edition of one thousand. Interestingly, it is Iosa Ghini himself who appears in the advertisement. One is not just buying the sunglasses, but is buying into the image of the designer.

In tandem with his many designs are Iosa Ghini's drawings. The drawings depict entire bolidist environments. They are full of action, frozen moments passing through Iosa Ghini's mind, a world of his own creation. The moments are captured in a cartoonlike mode; in fact, Iosa Ghini started drawing cartoons professionally in the early 1980s. His cartoons depicted the adventures of a living engineer, whom he transformed into Captain Eduardo Alberto Sillavengo. Cartoons led to television set design, where Iosa Ghini was, in fact, creating furniture, as well as fragments of imagined buildings. As he has moved further into actual interior and furniture design, the imagined places have become reality. Today, Iosa Ghini still uses drawing as investigation; his *Fluid City* series of drawings represents a city linked by communication rather than physical means. But what is the language of communication? In Iosa Ghini's drawings the communication seems to be, as the name suggests, fluid. Pulsing bands of moving energy cut through his drawings, as if to say that this communication will be a continual blur of visual data, signs, images, passing at split-second intervals, a visual white noise. Iosa Ghini's designs give structure to a phenomenon of communication, which in many ways already exists. This is, of course, the point of his design work: to address ways in which design can communicate in a more united Europe.

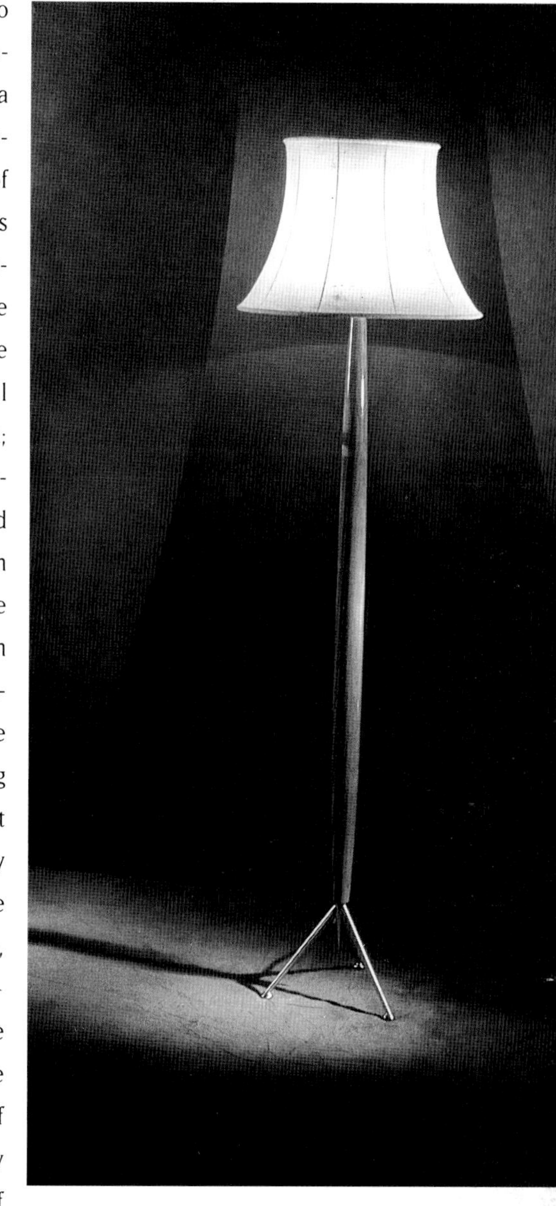

Opposite: *Numero 1* armchair from the *Dinamic* collection, Massimo Iosa Ghini, 1987, manufactured by Moroso. Photograph courtesy of Moroso.

Above: *Curzio* floor lamp, Massimo Iosa Ghini, 1991, produced in a limited edition by Lisar. Photograph courtesy of Stilnuova.

Above: *Balzo 5* two-seat sofa from the *Dinamic* collection, Massimo Iosa Ghini, 1987, manufactured by Moroso. Photograph courtesy of Moroso.

Right: Carpet, Massimo Iosa Ghini, 1991, produced in a limited edition for Galerie Yves Gastou. Photograph courtesy of Galerie Yves Gastou.

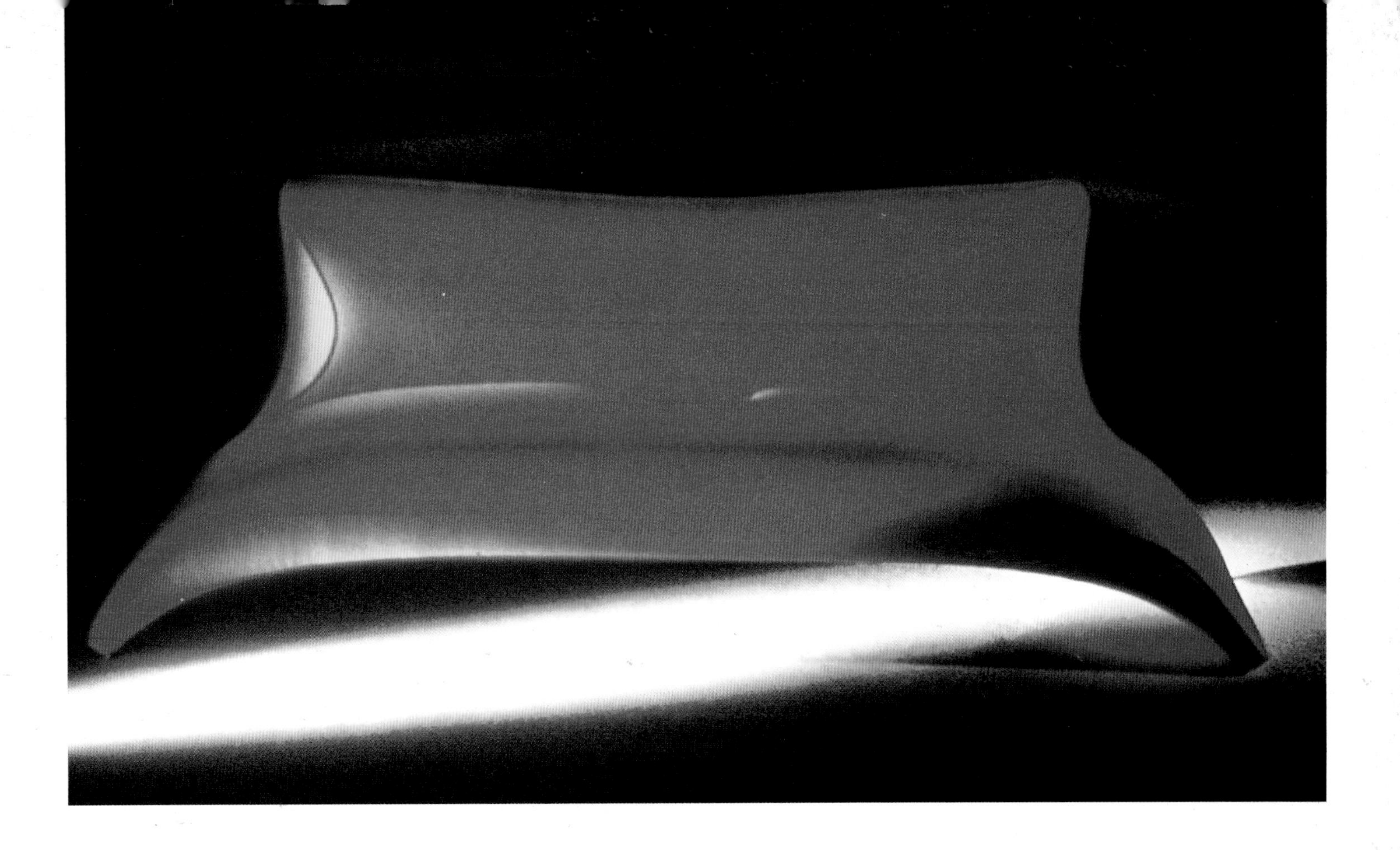

Iosa Ghini's furniture designs are an outgrowth of his drawn worlds and a means to bring the same ideas to reality. They have lines to make movement easier; they eradicate the friction and keep things flexible, sliding, flowing. The idea of constant movement and interaction is Iosa Ghini's challenge to a world which, he believes, has become sedentary; his means are the signs of man's most sedentary moments: the chair, the table. His strategy is to turn the tables, to make the sedentary the active.

Above: *Boomerang* sofa, Massimo Iosa Ghini, 1989, manufactured by Moroso. Photograph courtesy of Neotu.

Below: *Tobosa* table, Massimo Iosa Ghini, circa 1989, produced for The Design Gallery. Photograph courtesy of Neotu.

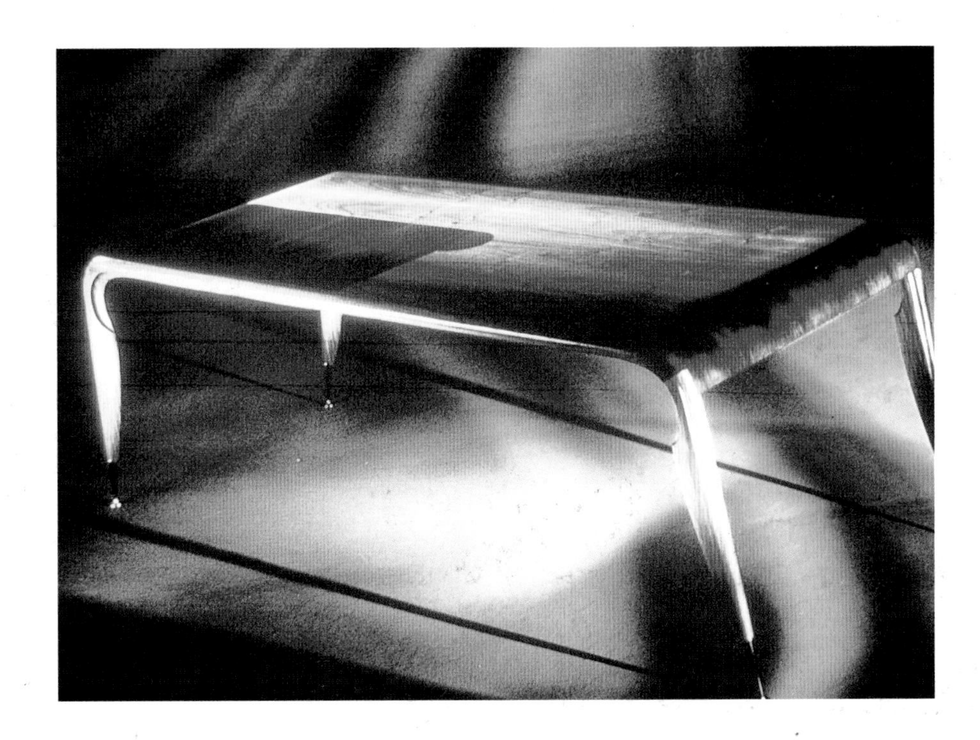

Above: *Minerva* pier-glass, Massimo Iosa Ghini, 1991, produced in a limited edition for Lisar. Photograph courtesy of Stilnuova.

Opposite: *Bonaparte* desk, Massimo Iosa Ghini, 1991, produced in a limited edition by Lisar. Photograph courtesy of Stilnuova.

Left: *Omero* coatrack, Massimo Iosa Ghini, 1991, produced in a limited edition by Lisar. Photograph courtesy of Stilnuova.

Below: *Fluens* wardrobe, Massimo Iosa Ghini, 1991, produced in a limited edition for Lisar. Photograph courtesy of Stilnuova.

Opposite: *Ponza* sideboard, Massimo Iosa Ghini, 1991, produced in a limited edition by Lisar. Photograph courtesy of Stilnuova.

Above: *Number 35* and *Number 36* concave armchairs of zinc-coated steel with tin rods and panels, Rei Kawakubo, 1991, produced by Comme des Garçons. Photograph courtesy of Comme des Garçons.

While Iosa Ghini is bold extroversion, Rei Kawakubo moves intuitively in silence and rigor. She also exists within the realm of the New Baroque, in its most modern mode of "continuous performance."[13] Her work—the clothing she designs for her company, Comme des Garçons, designs of her boutiques, and furniture design—is at every point an event. She has designed furniture since 1983, approaching this aspect of design with the same appetite for images and the same dexterity in the manipulation of form and materials that typifies her clothing. The emotion is seen in chairs such as *Number 24,* formed by a spiraling line of tubular steel which seems to continue into infinity. Kawakubo is not a clothing designer turned furniture designer but a designer who has embraced the totality of possibilities under the name of Comme des Garçons. Each phase of her design work can be, and has been, described as indisputably modern. It is indeed modern, yet always evolving and not frozen in time or style.

The furniture forms an ensemble with the clothing and the boutique designs. Says Kawakubo, "I've always attempted to create as complete an environment as possible for my clothes, so furniture was a natural progression."[14] For her furniture, she works with Toshiaki Oshiba, who interprets her ideas into forms. These ideas are expressed by speech and gesture; their essence comes to the fore without reams of sketches. The process of design concentrates on the ability to express a felt concept; it becomes choreography, the structuring of an idea through thought, gesture, and motion. Involved in producing collections in menswear and women's clothing, overseeing boutique designs, creating furniture, and publishing the magazine *Six,* Kawakubo is the ideal Renaissance woman who never existed in the Renaissance.

Above: *Number 32* quarter chair of tin, Rei Kawakubo, 1991, produced by Comme des Garçons. Photograph courtesy of Comme des Garçons.

Left: *Number 29* quarter chair of tin with lacquer-finish seat, Rei Kawakubo, 1991, produced by Comme des Garçons. Photograph courtesy of Comme des Garçons.

Below: *Number 27* chair with French Regency frame in beech and seat and back in brass, Rei Kawakubo, 1990, produced by Comme des Garçons. Photograph courtesy of Comme des Garçons.

Above and Left:
Number 28 chairs with French Regency frame in natural beech and seat and back in brass, Rei Kawakubo, 1990, produced by Comme des Garçons. Photographs courtesy of Comme des Garçons.

Above: Comme des Garçons furniture showroom, rue Marché Saint Honoré, Paris, 1991. Photograph by Jean Pierre Godeaut, courtesy of Comme des Garçons.

In 1990, Kawakubo appropriated a French Regency style for a collection of chairs. Why the sudden move to a known historic silhouette, albeit with the unknown surprise of a brass seat and back? Kawakubo's designs have always been imaginative, exploring new fabrics, forms, and moods. She has been presenting her designs in Paris since 1981, bringing images of Europe into her diverse vocabulary; recently, the clothing has been photographed in the romantic settings of old theaters and misty European hills. Her newest furniture and clothing designs are decidedly the product of an increasingly borderless world. The 1991 collection, largely in tin, was inspired by an attraction to the tin buckets and cups found in bazaars. "Beyond the ethnic feeling I have for tin," says Kawakubo, speaking of the *Number 32* chair, "I had an impulse to add something modern to this chair, so I added the aluminum chains. It was more of a sensual impulse." This type of impulse is typical of Kawakubo's internal/external approach to design.

Acting on her personal passion for art as well as design, Rei Kawakubo has long exhibited the work of other artists in her various boutiques. The intervention of the artists creates overlapping dialogues with both the space, embodying the image of Comme des Garçons, and the spectator. In the fall of 1991, it was Alessandro Mendini, the master of Italian design, who came to intervene in the rue Etienne Marcel boutique in Paris. After seeing Mendini's "Interior of an Interior," installation in the gallery Dilmos in Milan, Kawakubo was intrigued with the concept of using a single idea, in this case a type of pointillism, to completely transcend an interior and achieve what Mendini calls, "a mental interior: the interior of an interior." In Paris, Mendini repeated the same theme in an original installation, which was interesting for having created a new forum in which the work of two designers is found within the same space, in an exchange not of objects but of ideas.

Below: "Interior of an Interior" installation, Comme des Garçons boutique, rue Etienne Marcel, Paris, August—October 1991, designed by Alessandro Mendini. Photograph courtesy of Comme des Garçons.

Existing for the present, being shaped by the present, is the essential quality of the New Moderns. It is a given that through one's career the direction of one's work will change, altering course as new impressions, new questions, become important. Each design, however, will always be of that designer at that moment, a marker of event and being, a modern design. Looking at the range of a designer's work, such as that of architect/designer Volker Albus, shows just how timely and divergent those changes are. In Albus's "Molto Decadente" installation of 1987, he created a baroque bordello with his red folding screen, chandelier, and puffy stool. It was a direction he felt well worth exploring in the late 1980s. In the 1990s, he turned to more amorphic shapes: lamps of blown glass left in globular shapes, and red and volcanic walls for a boutique. Each setting, however, contains Albus's interest in spaces that hold a message and have a certain animation, concepts which Albus feels are important in his industrialized and sometimes cold homeland.

Above: "Molto Decadente" installation, designed by Volker Albus, 1987, for the Gallery Pentagon, Cologne, with *Avant Après* folding screen, *Weaner Blut* chandelier, and *Lido* stool, produced by the artist. Photograph by Bernhard Schaub.

Opposite: Interior of the Ria Leslau accessory boutique, designed by Volker Albus with Reinhard Müller and Barbara Szüts, 1991. Photograph by Andreas Schmidt.

There is an increasing concern with intimacy in much of the New Modern design. There are no leanings towards a mega-scale, an overall uniformity which will unite the modern world. On the contrary, these designs are personal, changing in mood from design to design, from one episode to the

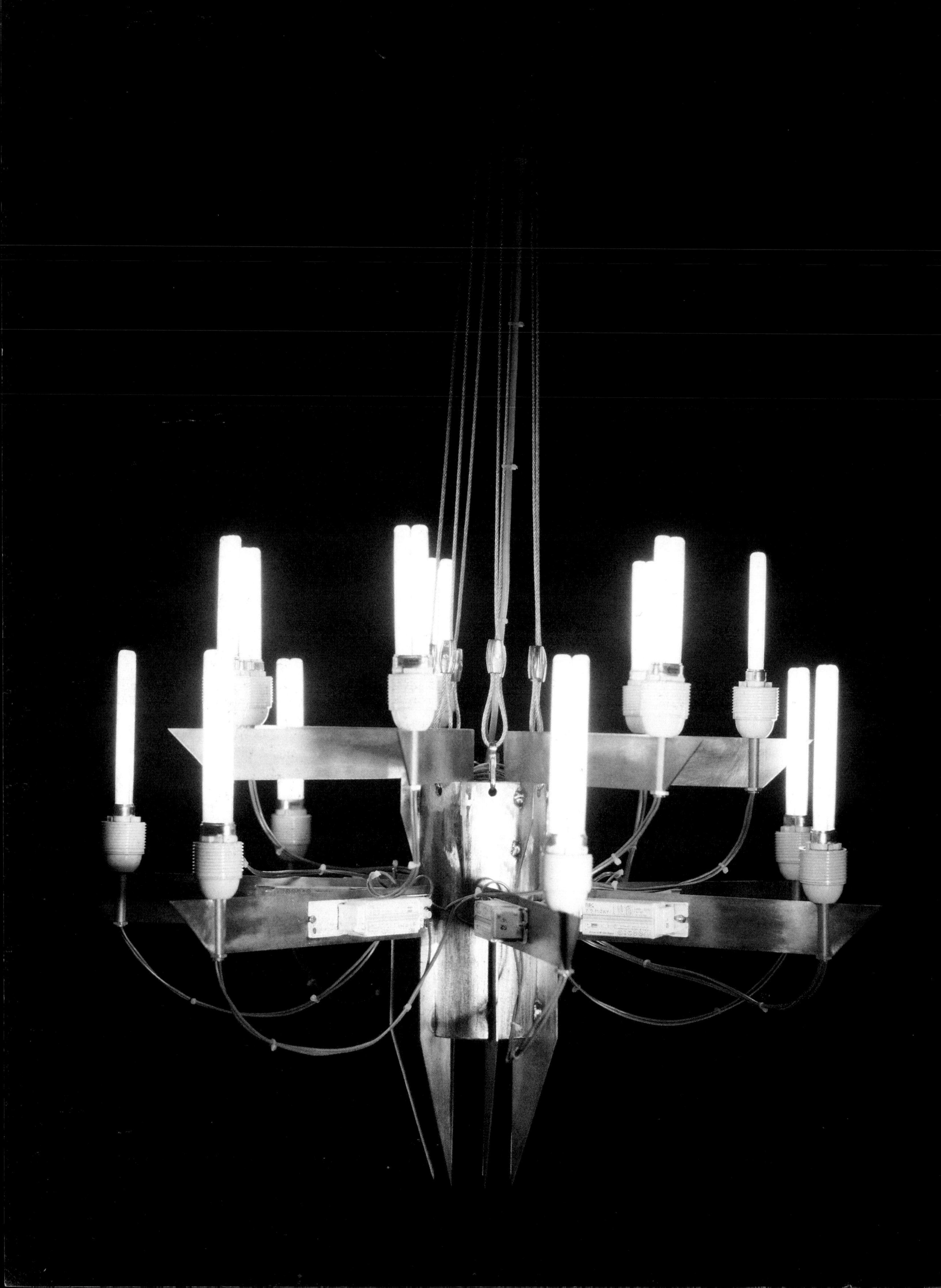

Above: *Freisitz Mollinissimo* chair, Volker Albus, 1991, produced by the artist. Photograph courtesy of Volker Albus.

Opposite: *Weaner Blut* chandelier, Volker Albus, 1987, produced in a limited edition for the artist. Photograph by Bernhard Schaub.

next. As the designs become more human, they also need to tie into the flowing system of intra-European and international communication. It is at this level that the making of visual messages becomes important to correlate with a world of computer graphics and electronics, the fax and video. One can communicate to the world from a very small, very intimate space; two levels or more of modernity can coexist simultaneously. The New Modern is a design that seeks to have it all.

Post-Punk Romantic

As the 1970s began to recede, a dissatisfaction arose, a rebelliousness against the deification of the object. What had the purity of line and form done to enrich or even touch upon the day-to-day rituals of living? Modern man would not find a brave new existence through a machine that homogenized but through the engagement of other machines—those of communication. Since the 1970s, media and image production have had obvious effects that must be dealt with in the physical environment. Efforts arose in art, literature, and the design schools, first to expose the effects of evasive layers of communication, and then to find ways to infiltrate the system. First came Paper Architecture and the developing of verbal weapons for reform, followed by the urge to make things happen, guerilla movements—acts of urban intervention from artists and designers alike. "To some extent, the Modern movement's to blame," says architect Nigel Coates. "When it should have stressed movement, more often than not it created a banal emphasis of the artifact." This emphasis on the artifact, on something cherished in and of itself, was not enough to fill the voids of modernity or to tie in to what Jean Baudrillard would call the "ecstasy of communication."

Design had taken itself very seriously. But another culture was forming by the 1980s, one which merged with media, event, art, and action. As Nigel Coates notes, "The worlds of music and magazines, fashion and furniture design began to cross over. They were not so concerned with proving the autonomy of their own fields as with being sophisticated amateurs. A spirit of collaboration was in the air. Artists made videos for fashion shows, singers made chairs. Industry was anathema."[15] Many of the individuals who began to design during this period, desiring to touch the public with their work and to collaborate on a broad basis with other artists, have an innate ability to utilize the tools of the media to their benefit.

Amidst the crossing currents of making, drawing, and verbalizing, the parameters of design have blurred. Is furniture design the exclusive territory of those trained in the field? Or, more important, in today's culture how can those trained as designers merge their talents with those of the fashion, music, and print worlds to arrive at a design of multiple layers—a design with mass communication capabilities? It is no accident that many of the designers in this book began their careers with projects such as clubs, restaurants, and boutiques—projects where they are instantly in touch with a public in fashion and high consumption.

Nigel Coates experienced firsthand the changes in design through the 1970s and 1980s, first as a student at London's Architecture Association, then as a professor, and as a practicing architect with Doug Branson in Branson Coates Architecture, with whom he works to this day. Coates first caught attention with his magazine/manifesto, *NATO* (Narrative Architecture Today); he then went to Japan, where his bold, "not-to-be-missed" designs were ideal for a society that consumes images at an alarming rate. In fact, Coates might have made himself too consumable. After all, by satisfying an image-hungry culture isn't the designer likely to be consumed, and disposed of, himself? Certainly, his famous Caffè Bongo in Tokyo has already been altered, its original image neutered and its wings clipped, after only five years of existence. Design today is less and less a permanent art. Designers such as Philippe Starck have shown the way to maximize exposure with good design for the fashion-conscious. However, as all great designers, Starck understands when to be consumable for gluttony's sake and when to be enduring. Nigel Coates will continue to take on challenging architectural commissions, each a new testing ground, with plenty of energy left over for furniture and interior design.

Opposite: *Massaï* chair (detail), Kristian Gavoille, 1990, produced in a limited edition for Neotu. Photograph by Karin Knoblich.

Coates relies on a mix of visual imagery to recount the unique narrative within each interior space. His interiors are collaborations with various artists, including Tom Dixon and André Dubreuil. His design sketches read like layered stage sets, full of movement. His furniture is provocative. His work has been called baroque for its inventiveness and theatricality, and Industrial Baroque (by Coates himself) for its process and movement. One sees the influence of the fashion world in his work on projects for Katharine Hamnett and Jasper Conran, and in his ability to mix meanings and influences. Each project becomes a visual feast; the observer is thrust into the action of the art of shopping and of the theater of amusements and heroics.

Coates's design for the Caffè Bongo looks as if the modern world had crash-landed into a baroque bordello. With an airplane wing hanging over the entry, seeming to penetrate the interior, Coates made a literal sign of the dynamic in his design. The idea of movement, of traveling through time and space, is present in most of Coates's work. It's felt in the design's conception as he flies through drawings as if creating a story board for a film, as well as in the details of the lines of the space, in the furniture of his own design. Standing in a Coates interior gives one the feeling of being in the center of a space that has been spun around a few times and then stopped by a knowing hand when the mix was right. In Katharine Hamnett's Sloane Street boutique, a wall of fish tanks divides interior from exterior; looking into the store past the theatrical drapes and aquariums (a fetish of Ms. Hamnett's), one is not sure whether to be observer or player.

Even without the associative enclosure of his interiors, Coates's furniture designs have their own spirit of communication and involvement with the user. Says Coates, "I want our work to avoid the objectivity of so much twentieth-century architecture and design, in favor of making fields of potential meaning that are activated by the user." Since 1988, in his designs for Poltronova (chairs whose backs wrap around like scrolls), in the *Gallo Galleggio Gallino Gallone* group of upholstered chairs, a sofa, and tables (see "The New Naturalism"), and in the *Genie* stool originally designed for the restaurant L'Arca di Noè in Sapporo, Japan, and now manufactured by SCP, there has always been a very human, if not sexual, side. He also repeats the theme of tension, the idea of stretching the covering, which started with the *Jazz* chair, and has been taken further in the designs for the Turkish discotheque Taxim, where the soft upholstery is stretched like a glove over the form. His evolution, from his beginnings in English design to his current projects with the large Italian manufacturers, is not just one of form or image, but of process.

Coates talks of design in England today as "survival" in an aesthetically hostile society: "[It] comes from making do, street culture, and an established eccentric tradition in England. In England

Opposite: Wooden chairs, Nigel Coates, 1991, manufactured by Poltronova. Photograph courtesy of Poltronova.

Below: Chair and stools from the *Noah* collection, Nigel Coates, 1988, manufactured by SCP. Photograph by Lynn Werner.

Above: *Genie* stool from the *Noah* collection, Nigel Coates, 1988, produced by the artist. Photograph courtesy of Branson Coates Architecture.

Right: *Jazz* chair, Branson Coates Architecture, 1986, manufactured by Rockstone. Photograph courtesy of Branson Coates Architecture.

Opposite: Katharine Hamnett boutique, Sloane Street, London, designed by Nigel Coates, 1988, with ceiling light fixtures by Patrice Butler. Photograph by Patrice Butler.

it was a matter of not having an industry or a design school, or great 'gods' of design." English designers worked it out for themselves. It was often a question of "harnessing the way society was set up to do things," says Coates. This approach allowed them to adapt their work to the existing technology. They ended up "hijacking" the English tradition of furniture production; the method used for the chairs of L'Arca di Noè, for example, adapted the system set up for the classic Windsor chair. They produced not an abstraction of an existing design, but an "exploitation."

Exploitation is a constant of 1990s production. One studies the way society is accustomed to absorbing information. This is certainly true in the world of fashion, which understands that it is selling not only a shirt on a wire hanger, but a shirt that engages a fantasy. To do this, clothing designers have also taken to orchestrated environments for their own shops, to sell design through design. One memorable and changing space is that of Moschino Haute Couture on Via S. Andrea in Milan. Too wild to be called classic—yet full of painted clouds, velvet swags, and curvaceous furniture—the brashness of this boutique and of Franco Moschino himself can be called the punk of *haut chic*. His boutique is a stage set for the art of shopping. The design is literally a theater, with a stair giving a sense of false perspective to the depth of the stage and where curtains pull back to reveal the clothes which are, of course, the stars. Moschino is best known as a maverick designer of clothing who often makes fun of the fashion industry, writing slogans such as "Expensive Jacket" on the backs of his designs. For those jaded with design, this boutique is a heaven on earth, lush and full of art metaphors.

Above: "Atelier Haute Coupure!" display, Moschino shop, Via S. Andrea, Milan, April 17 through May 28, 1989. Photograph courtesy of Moschino.

Opposite: Magritte-inspired display, Moschino shop, Via S. Andrea, Milan, 1989. Photograph courtesy of Moschino.

MOSCHINO

Above: "Ceci n'est pas une boutique" window display, Moschino shop, Via S. Andrea, Milan, May 29 through July 15, 1989. Photograph courtesy of Moschino.

Right: Window display, Moschino shop, Via Durini, Milan, July—August 1991. Photograph courtesy of Moschino.

Opposite: "Colomba Magritte" display, Moschino shop, Via S. Andrea, Milan, February 17 through April 2, 1991. Photograph courtesy of Moschino.

In his second Milan shop, on Via Durini, he wanted to create a supermarket for fashion. It has a sparser, more open plan of four hundred square meters, where the display of his jeans and ready-to-wear lines is on the rack, ready to be pulled down and put on. Throughout the two-story space he has placed red hearts, gold flounce, and glitz—logos of glamour—on railings or walls. They are not subtle—they are in fact tacky—but as Moschino is selling his line *Cheap and Chic* here, what better way to provide style and, very important, the experience of buying style, to the not so rich—yet.

Above: Interior of the Moschino shop, Via Durini, Milan, showing ground floor niche furnished in "antiques," 1990. Photograph courtesy of Moschino.

Opposite: "Ceci n'est pas une boutique" display, Moschino shop, Via S. Andrea, Milan, May 29 through July 15, 1989. Photograph courtesy of Moschino.

Above, top and Above, bottom: Window displays, Moschino shop, Via Durini, Milan, 1991. Photographs courtesy of Moschino.

Opposite: "Gigli" window display, Moschino shop, Via S. Andrea, Milan, May 1991. Photograph courtesy of Moschino.

Above: *Tippi Girl* chair, Anne Liberati and Joris Heetman, 1989, produced for Chaperon & Méchant Loup. Photograph courtesy of Anne Liberati and Joris Heetman.

Spinning at a fast rhythm off the worlds of fashion design, dance, art, with a post-1960s-generation consciousness is the collection *Pom-Pom Girls* of Anne Liberati and Joris Heetman. Full of furniture which begs to be played with, the collection entices and flirts. The cabinets *Pin-up* and *Bric à Brac* are wrapped in curtains, pulled back to expose the drawers. Along with the laced-up leather table legs of *Wanda,* the designs seem almost pornographic in the constrained world of furniture design. The design team, who work between Paris and Amsterdam, describe their furniture as having a personality, a sensuality, an imagination that is more out of Alice in Wonderland than traditional academic theories. The personas expressed in the *Pom-Pom Girls* collection are alive with movement. The fabric curtains on the cabinets rustle and the metal curtains create a soft music as one walks by. These are the personas of the circus and the cabaret. It is an interaction of ideas brought from a variety of mediums and solutions formed from a variety of materials. The problem of materials is dealt with as an extension of the emerging personality. The designers ask themselves, how does one develop and express the potentialities? How does one rediscover the lost techniques? The forms are from a known category of furniture: chairs, tables, cabinets, all recognizable as those objects. It is, say the designers, "a redressing of the basic objects . . . . A chair is a chair; it is a question of point of view."

The Liberati-Heetman point of view is one that puts the viewer in contact with the object. In mass-produced furniture, five coats of paint might be applied for an indestructible lacquer finish; in these pieces, perhaps only one is used, forcing the user to put on a coat of wax, thereby creating a reason to interact with the furniture. Gone is the period of the exclusive object, the object that only speaks within itself of a closed set of design rules and theories. The cultural climate today is one of "a simple vision," says Liberati. It is also one which is less trapped by borders.

Producing their creations under their own company, Chaperon & Méchant Loup (taken from the story of Little Red Riding Hood, the name is meant to convey the relationship between the mischievous imp and the nasty wolf, roles which are interchanged during the process of design), Liberati and Heetman make no compromises. They began with an idea, built prototypes, and then went around to the galleries where they were given shows. They oversee all facets of the process. Although each piece can be produced in a large series, a consideration ingrained in Heetman's background as an industrial designer, they began with limited series pieces out of necessity—to get the pieces out. They have gone on from *Pom-Pom Girls* to create other collections. An upcoming collection for Nobilis in Paris will be a family of coverable chairs, ottomans, and the like; called *Lola,* the collection is dressable in Nobilis's own fabrics. Another collection, with the theme *Temperance,* was created during a month's stay as invited artists at the Fondation Beychevelle. The seven-piece collection includes a stepladder that resembles two legs in full stride when extended, with the hinge at the hip joint. It also includes a new cabinet, this time decorated in laser-cut, opaque, colored Plexiglas. The collection presents an *esthétique d'existence,* which, according to the designers, is more "an art than a moral code."

Above: *Wanda* table (detail), Anne Liberati and Joris Heetman, 1989, produced for Chaperon & Méchant Loup. Photograph courtesy of Anne Liberati and Joris Heetman.

Below: Sketch of *Bric à Brac* cabinet for Chaperon & Méchant Loup, Anne Liberati and Joris Heetman, 1990. Photograph courtesy of Anne Liberati and Joris Heetman.

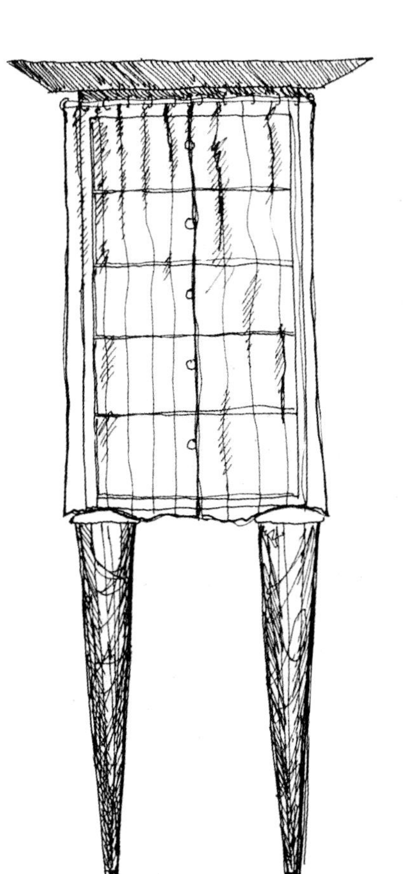

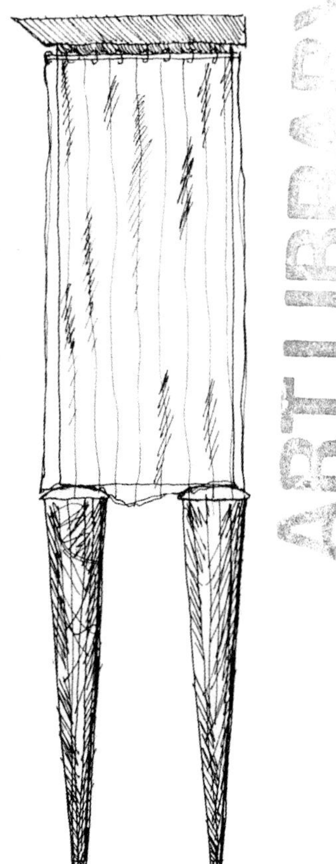

Opposite: *Pin-Up* cabinet, Anne Liberati and Joris Heetman, 1990, produced for Neotu and Chaperon & Méchant Loup. Photograph courtesy of Neotu.

Below: *Anna* table, Anne Liberati and Joris Heetman, 1989, produced for Chaperon & Méchant Loup. Photograph courtesy of Anne Liberati and Joris Heetman.

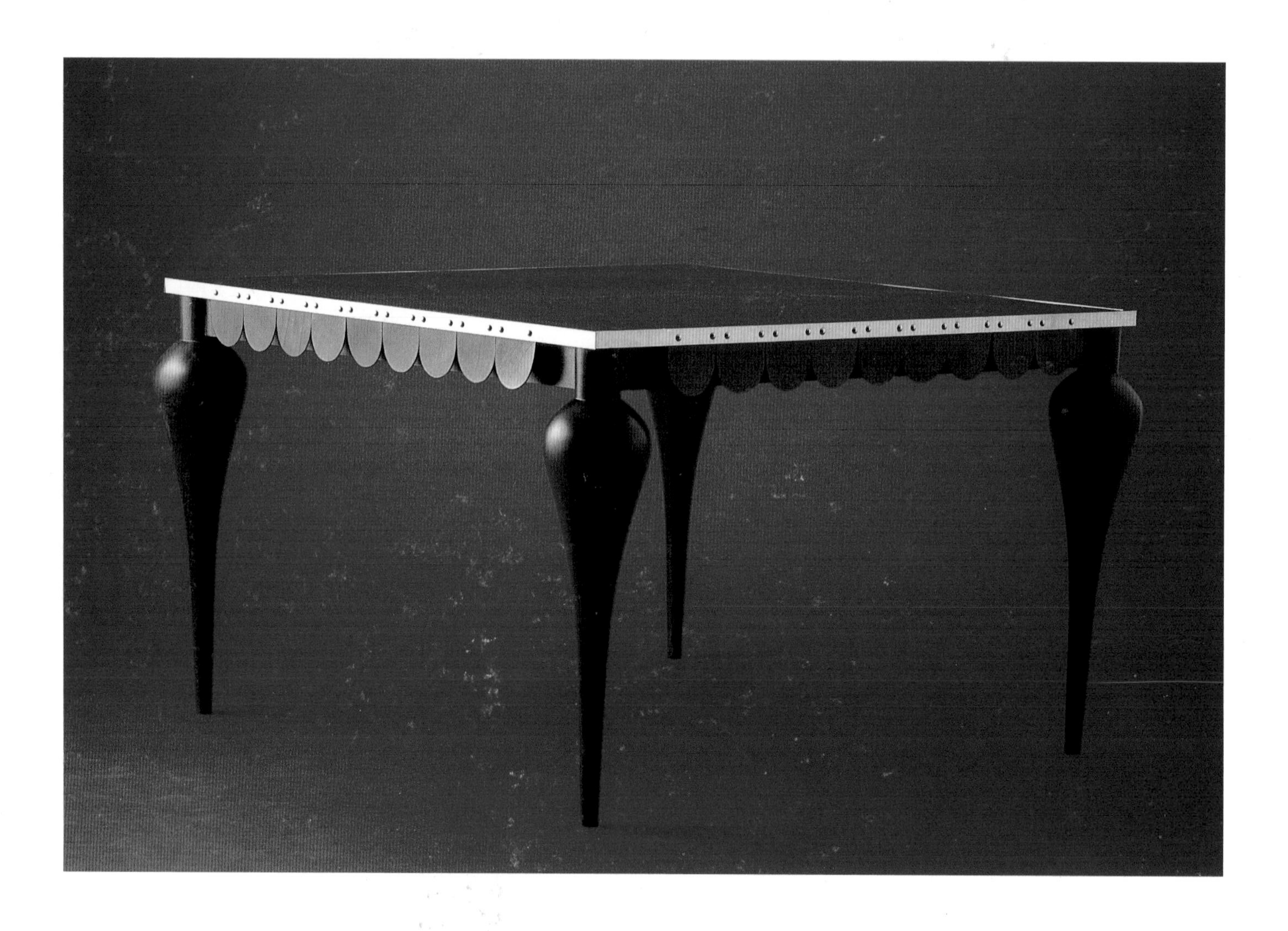

Left: *Merlino* elastic lamp, Karim Azzabi, 1990, manufactured by Oceano Oltreluce. Photograph courtesy of Oceano Oltreluce.

Existence, in this Post-Punk, after-the-party age, has often meant staying in, staying safe, economizing; it has also seen a return of family fun and inspired social consciousness. Oceano Oltreluce has brought out one of the few lamps that defines the Post-Punk Romantic world. Much as Richard Sapper's *Tizio* lamp for Artemide captured the 1970s and part of the 1980s as a much-envied object and a symbol of design literacy, so do the elastic lamps by Karim Azzabi capture the 1990s, with all of its small thrills and quiet revolutions. These lamps are inventive, fun, and not that useful, except, of course, for setting a mood and glowing in the dark. These lamps, as so much in the 1990s, recall images of the 1960s without the politics. They could be found alongside inflatable furniture and lamps filled with psychedelic colored liquids. The elastic lamps, in four shapes and four Day-Glo colors, are of the latest inflatable PVC, and are interchangeable on their aluminum bases. They are, in a word, clever.

Left: *Fiaccola* elastic lamp, Karim Azzabi, 1990, manufactured by Oceano Oltreluce. Photograph courtesy of Oceano Oltreluce.

Below: *Anelli* elastic lamp, Karim Azzabi, 1990, manufactured by Oceano Oltreluce. Photograph courtesy of Oceano Oltreluce.

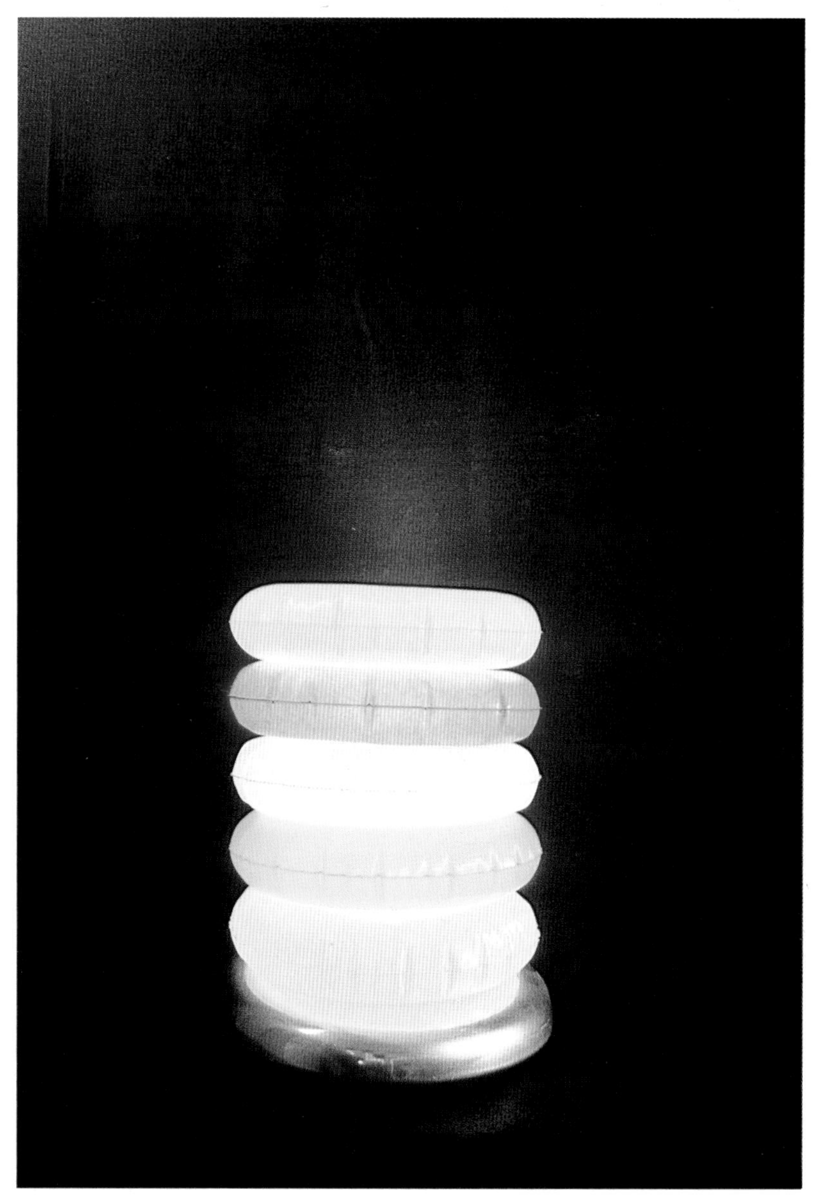

Above: Lamps from the *Affolé* collection, Philippe Renaud and Patrice Gruffaz, 1990, produced for Galerie Lieux and Etamine. Photograph by J. Clapot.

The *Affolé* lamps by Philippe Renaud and Patrice Gruffaz for Galerie Lieux and Etamine, with their springing metal spines and paper lampshades, and the more serious *Ecate* by Toni Cordero for Artemide are some of the few other lamps to have made a memorable impression on the 1990s. The *Affolé*, simple and affordable fun, is a sort of first step into design. The *Ecate* makes use of industrial design and current culture to actually rethink what a lamp is, what a lampshade is, and the quality of light. Here, it should be noted, the designers are not as young as their designs, but then neither is Johnny Rotten, or any 1970s icon who made it to the 1990s.

Above: *Ecate* table lamp, Toni Cordero, 1990, manufactured by Artemide. Photograph courtesy of Artemide.

Left: *Anchise* floor lamp, Toni Cordero, 1990, manufactured by Artemide. Photograph courtesy of Artemide.

Right: *Midinette* table, Kristian Gavoille, 1988, prototype produced for VIA. Photograph courtesy of VIA.

Below: *Mademoiselle* table, Kristian Gavoille, 1988, prototype produced for VIA. Photograph courtesy of VIA.

Below: *Monalysa* chair, Kristian Gavoille, 1990, prototype produced for VIA. Photograph courtesy of VIA.

covering, reminiscent of one at Grandma's house seen through technicolor lenses. Is Gavoille's generation finding a needed tranquillity at home, or do they just have a desire to express the home environment? After all, could one ever really put the plastic fruit on the International Style glass table or let the dog loose near the Le Corbusier lounge? Was it all too unreal for the designers of the 1990s?

If the International Style seemed unreal in terms of expectations, the designs of the Post-Punk Romantic generation often seem unreal in terms of context. For whose home are they? Most of these designs have a movement, depth of color, and an animation that seem to have jumped out of a television set. Does that make them for imaginary people and situations? No. It only shows that most interiors are out of touch with the everyday reality of television and other image productions of the

Above: *Dédérenée* rolling bar, Kristian Gavoille, 1990, prototype produced for VIA. Photograph courtesy of VIA.

While many young designers are trying to shake things up, Kristian Gavoille appears to be letting things cool down—but not too much. His furniture and object designs are for the quiet evening at home, reflection, memories of a happy moment, a picnic, a meeting with friends. Not that Gavoille is the reticent type. A past punk-clubber and rebel, he has recently finished four years in the office of Philippe Starck. During this time, he was working on his own furniture designs, exhibiting at Neotu in Paris, and designing sets for television and concerts. Inspired by fashion, the skirts of Chantal Thomass to be specific, he designed the *Divine*, a wooden table with a full metal skirt at its base. This design was a precursor of many which would be either dressed up or in other ways given an animated quality. Later, his *Massaï* chair was more animal and certainly a bolder design than his earlier works. Now, as creative director of Ardi, he is working on the small, intimate object for the home.

Gavoille was awarded a Carte Blanche (basically an endowment) from VIA, which allowed him to create a new collection of furniture. The result, exhibited at the 1991 International Furniture Fair in Paris, is a collection of characters: an armoire shaped into a trunk with lip-shaped cutouts for handles, designs entitled *Conchita* and *Plaisir d'A*, and a small yellow armchair with a napkinlike

Right: *Divine* table, Kristian Gavoille, 1987, produced for Neotu. Photograph by Karin Knoblich.

Right: *Falbalas* lamp, Kristian Gavoille, 1988, prototype produced for VIA. Photograph courtesy of VIA.

media. Rather than be helplessly absorbed into a world which already surrounds us, some designers have chosen to join in, to create communicable environments.

Gavoille's creations are themselves not too far in appearance and feel from the set of the television show "Pee-wee's Playhouse." Some of the resemblance is due to shared experience; Gavoille and many other designers in this book have worked closely with the fields of music and set design. The other factor is that, in the 1980s and 1990s, the most original creation has been taking place in the fields of video, computer graphics, and film—areas in which new technology has provided the only fresh territory for designers. The moving, talking chair of Pee-wee Herman, as well as the incredible lighting, props, and costumes of a Madonna stage set are truly innovative and original. They are clearly products of minds raised on television. Such designs show the ability of the designer to create action in

Opposite: *Atheo* chair, Kristian Gavoille, 1989, produced in a limited edition for Neotu. Photograph by Karin Knoblich.

Right: *Conchita* chair, Kristian Gavoille, 1990, prototype produced for VIA. Photograph courtesy of VIA.

Below: *14 Juillet au Soir* (the night of July 14) table with suspended lamps, Kristian Gavoille, 1990, prototype produced for VIA. Photograph courtesy of VIA.

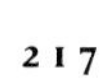

Above: *Massaï* chair, Kristian Gavoille, 1990, produced in a limited edition for Neotu. Photograph by Karin Knoblich.

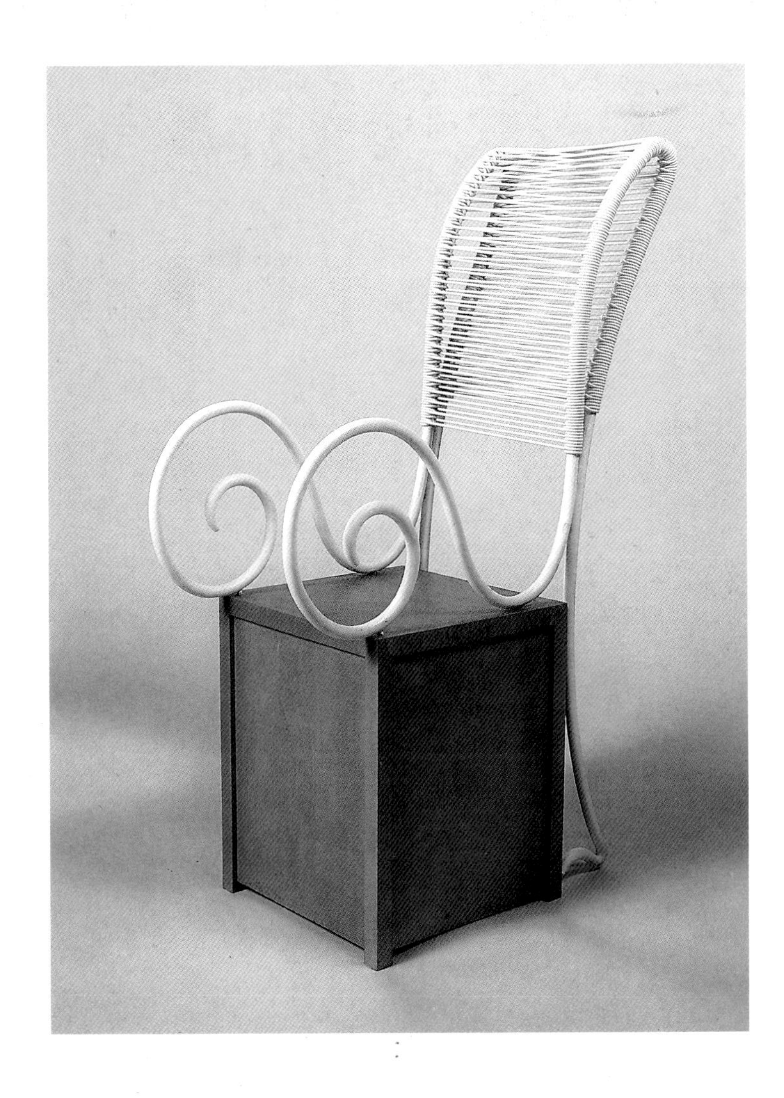

Left: *Plaisir d'A* chair, Kristian Gavoille, 1990, prototype produced for VIA. Photograph courtesy of VIA.

Below: *Memoialor* armoire, Kristian Gavoille, 1990, prototype produced for VIA. Photograph courtesy of VIA.

three-dimensional forms, in one-act interiors that completely express a moment or sentiment. They are spaces that manipulate the user/viewer, as they are quickly changed for each scenario life offers. Designers would often like to have this magical ability to create continually flowing interiors; so far, they have succeeded in substituting the event for the autonomy of the object. Of course, as the media also uses art and design for inspiration, the cycle is complete—one field learning from the other.

Notes

Introduction

1. Andrea Branzi and François Burkhardt, Exhibit Manifesto, "Capitales Européennes du Nouveau Design: Barcelone, Düsseldorf, Milan, Paris," Centre Georges Pompidou, March 6–27, 1991.

2. Ibid.

3. Ibid.

4. Paul Rabinow, ed., *The Foucault Reader* (New York: Pantheon Books, 1984).

5. All quotes by John B. Jackson from "The Purpose of the City: Changing City Landscapes as Manifestations of Cultural Values," in *The Architect and the City,* Papers from the AIA ACSA Teacher Seminar, Cranbrook Academy of Art, June 11–12, 1962, ed. Marcus Whitten (Cambridge: The MIT Press, 1962).

The New Baroque

6. John Summerson, *The Architecture of the Eighteenth Century* (London: Thames and Hudson, 1986), 10.

7. Christian Norberg-Schulz, *The Baroque Age* (Paris: Berger-Levrault, 1979), 12.

8. Ibid.

The New Naturalism

9. Andrea Branzi, *Domestic Animals, The Neo-primitive Style* (Cambridge: The MIT Press, 1987), chapter 2.

10. Stefano Casciani, *Furniture As Architecture, Design & Zanotta Products* (Milan: Arcadia Edizioni, 1988), 160.

Bricolage

11. Ron Arad, "The City and Some Thing (Neo-nothing: Post All)," in *Ron Arad,* ed. Alexander von Vegesack (Weil am Rhein: Vitra Design Museum, 1990), 15.

The New Modern

12. Borek Sípek, *Mamice—To My Mother* (Amsterdam: Steltman, 1990), 27.

13. Summerson, *The Architecture of the Eighteenth Century* (London: Thames and Hudson, 1986), 12.

14. Deyan Sudjic, *Rei Kawakubo and Comme des Garçons* (London: Fourth Estate, A Blueprint Monograph, 1990), 121.

Post-Punk Romantic

15. Nigel Coates, "The Codex is the City" (Lecture at the Tate Gallery, London, 1991).

Bibliography

Arad, Ron. "The City and Some Thing (Neo-nothing: Post All)." In *Ron Arad,* ed. Alexander von Vegesack. Weil am Rhein: Vitra Design Museum, 1990.

Branzi, Andrea. *Domestic Animals, The Neo-primitive Style.* Cambridge: The MIT Press, 1990.

Burkhardt, François and Eveno Claude, eds. *L'Etrange Univers de L'Architecte Carlo Mollino.* Paris: Centre Georges Pompidou, 1989.

Casciani, Stefano. *Furniture as Architecture, Design & Zanotta Products.* Milan: Arcadia Edizioni, 1988.

Coates, Nigel. "The Codex is the City." Lecture at the Tate Gallery, London, 1991.

Foucault, Michel. *The Foucault Reader,* ed. Paul Rabinow. New York: Pantheon Books, 1984.

Jackson, John B. "The Purpose of the City: Changing City Landscapes as Manifestations of Cultural Values." In *The Architect and the City,* ed. Marcus Whitten. (Papers from the AIA ACSA Teacher Seminar, Cranbrook Academy of Art, June 11–12, 1962). Cambridge: The MIT Press, 1962.

Norberg-Schulz, Christian. *The Baroque Age.* Paris: Berger-Levrault, 1979.

Poyner, Rick. *Nigel Coates: The City in Motion.* London: Fourth Estate, A Blueprint Monograph, 1989

Sípek, Borek. *Mamice—To My Mother.* Amsterdam: Steltman, 1990.

Sudjic, Dejan. *Rei Kawakubo and Comme des Garçons.* London: Fourth Estate, A Blueprint Monograph, 1990.

Summerson, John. *The Architecture of the Eighteenth Century.* London: Thames and Hudson, 1986.

Index

This book was designed on the Macintosh computer using Emigre's Matrix Book and Matrix Wide typefaces designed in 1985 by Zuzana Licko.